Leadership in Governance

Thomas W. Fryer, Jr.
John C. Lovas

Leadership
in
Governance

Creating Conditions
for Successful
Decision Making in the
Community College

 Jossey-Bass Publishers
San Francisco • Oxford • 1991

LEADERSHIP IN GOVERNANCE
*Creating Conditions for Successful Decision Making
in the Community College*
by Thomas W. Fryer, Jr., and John C. Lovas

Library of Congress Cataloging-in-Publication Data
Fryer, Thomas W., date.
Leadership in governance : creating conditions for successful
decision making in the community college / Thomas W. Fryer, Jr.,
John C. Lovas.
p.   cm. — (The Jossey-Bass higher and adult education series)
Includes bibliographical references and index.
ISBN 1-55542-321-3
1. Community colleges—United States—Administration.
2. Leadership. 3. Decision-making.   I. Lovas, John C., date.
II. Title.   III. Series.
LB2341.F79   1991   90—19201
378.1'07—dc 20

Manufactured in the United States of America

The paper in this book meets the guidelines for
permanence and durability of the Committee on
Production Guidelines for Book Longevity of the
Council on Library Resources.

JACKET DESIGN BY WILLI BAUM

FIRST EDITION

Code 9121

The Jossey-Bass
Higher and Adult
Education Series

Contents

Preface

"Tis the good reader that makes the good book."
—Ralph Waldo Emerson

The quest that led to the writing of this book was our effort to learn whether models of effective governance exist in local institutions and, if so, to identify and describe them. We have both been interested throughout our careers in questions of governance and leadership in community colleges. In *Leadership in Governance,* we offer the perspectives of practitioners. Our knowledge has been expanded by our research and reading in the literature; but we would be disingenuous if we claimed to base such authority as we may have solely on research and scholarship. In fact, we view our research and our findings in the literature through the lens of more than fifty years of experience in a variety of roles in a number of community colleges in several states. Thus, our experience constitutes the basic fund of knowledge upon which the book rests. This is a book by practitioners for practitioners. We hope it contains material that is useful for theory building, but we do not intend it to be a major contribution to the theoretical literature.

Our view of leadership and governance in community colleges diverges from more traditional analyses (Richardson, 1975; Deegan and Gollattscheck, 1985), although we share Deegan's hope that community colleges will "seek to make necessary decisions in a more comprehensive and integrated manner for the long-term welfare of the colleges" (1985, p. 81). Everyone in every institution makes decisions, and we see governance as a process that helps create the organizational climate within which those decisions are made. Through the exercise of leadership in governance, conditions are created that expand the extent to which individual decisions contribute to achieving the institution's purposes. Our approach holds that individuals play an important role in shaping decisions and that the inter-

personal behavior of those in positions of organizational authority is one facet of institutional governance. Those processes are
enormously complex, characterized by ambiguity and paradox
that must be recognized and managed. *Leadership in Governance* synthesizes our experience, our reading, and our studies
of internal governance in nine community college districts into
an accessible format that we hope readers will find thought-
provoking and useful.

We focus on the internal governance and leadership of
local institutions and do not address the important issues of
state-level governance, including those that derive from the
tensions between state and local interests. In many ways, however, these tensions gave rise to our particular attention to the
subject of local governance, as we explain in Chapter Two.

In recent years, many state-level bodies have developed
increasing confidence that they could govern local institutions more effectively from state capitals using state agencies
than could local boards and administrations. We find this
view particularly untimely. The best of the current literature
and research on organizational effectiveness deemphasizes
large, dominating central agencies; stresses empowering
people at the lowest organizational levels; and demonstrates
persuasively the crippling effects of trying to control through
bureaucratic rules and procedures.

Faith in the usefulness of central state control seems to
increase when money is scarce. This faith is strengthened
when atrocity stories from local institutions find their way
into the media. We have seen isolated incidents generalized
into a picture of local conditions as uniformly inefficient and
ineffective, thus requiring political remedies through state
law and regulation. Our experience, in contrast, suggests that,
for most decisions, the system that governs best is the system
that governs locally.

Audiences

Though we were guided in our work by several highly competent, well-respected educational researchers, we felt that pre-

senting our findings in a typical research monograph would not be appropriate. Rather, we believe our work will be more useful to practitioners, students, and others interested in the issues of leadership and governance in community colleges if it is presented in a form that blends our views of effective decision making and communication with examples from our research and insights from the literature.

As writers, we address this book to several audiences. We assume most readers will be people like ourselves—CEOs, trustees, teachers, administrators, staff members—who serve in community colleges and who wish those places to be effective institutions that are also good places in which to work. Other readers will be interested in higher education generally and in its complex forms of organization, or they will be practitioners who work at various levels of education but have an interest in effective decision making. Some, we hope, will be from fields entirely outside of education. As we explain in Chapter Two, the junior college was created in the twentieth century as a result of the high school moving up and the university moving down. Thus, in some respects, the modern community college resembles both the high school and the university. We believe practitioners from those segments will find our work relevant to their institutions as well.

Overview of the Chapters

Leadership in Governance reflects our conception of the elements that constitute effective decision making and communication in community colleges. We explain our conception of community colleges, their governance, and the idea of leadership in governance in Chapter One. Chapter Two delineates the complex nature of community colleges, suggesting the most important factors shaping the decision-making context. Chapter Three explains that clearly established and well-understood planning processes appear to be a critical element in sound internal decision making, particularly in budget development processes and in personnel decisions. Chapter Four shows how deciding permeates the institution, and it elaborates four aspects of decision making: context, preparation, structure and content, and participation. Chapter Five considers one of the less documented phenomena in internal governance processes: how various decisions are acted upon—that is, when and how they are implemented and what systems or methods are used to monitor their implementation. Chapter Six discusses decision making when the impulse for the decision comes from outside the routine processes of the organization, either from efforts at change and innovation by members or groups within the organization or from developments in the community or at the state level. Chapter Seven offers a description of such key concepts for successful organizational communication as redundancy, multiple channel, clarity, and credibility. Chapter Eight elaborates the key conceptual themes that emerge from our work and details a list of qualities that characterize successful decision making, providing a kind of checklist for practitioners.

At the end of each chapter we have provided a list of highlights. Readers may find it useful to begin each chapter by reading the highlights, which provide an overview of the material in the chapter. The institutional profiles in Resource A contain thumbnail sketches of the study institutions, which provide useful context for some of our examples.

Acknowledgments

This work would not have been successful without the help, advice, and support of a number of people. Most fundamentally, the trustees of the Foothill-De Anza Community College District—Raymond F. Bacchetti, Gerald Besson, Alfred P. Chasuk, Robert C. Smithwick, and Mary Wallace Wheat—provided district support, thereby recognizing the importance of documenting and describing good practice in American community colleges. In recognition of that support, all proceeds from the publication of this book will go to the Foothill-De Anza Colleges Foundation to support student scholarships.

Members of our study steering committee provided critical advice at every stage of the project. We are indebted to them for their practical suggestions and their warm support. The steering committee included Richard Axen, professor of education, San Francisco State University; Mark Edelstein, past president, Academic Senate of the California Community Colleges; Karen Sue Grosz, past president of the Academic Senate of the California Community Colleges; Ilona Katz, past president of the California Community College Trustees; James Kellerman, past president, Chief Executive Officers, California Community Colleges; Diana Lockard, trustee, Citrus College; John Petersen, executive director, Accrediting Commission for Community and Junior Colleges, Western Association of Colleges and Schools; John D. Randall, past president, Chief Executive Officers, California Community Colleges; Julie Slark, director of research, Rancho Santiago College; Larry Toy, past president, Faculty Association of California Community Colleges; David Viar, past executive director, California Community College Trustees; Daniel Weiler, partner in the policy research firm of Berman-Weiler Associates.

We were joined in our interviews of key decision makers by two superb researchers: Beryl Nelson, senior associate at Berman-Weiler Associates; and Janet Ruyle, assistant director, Center for Studies in Higher Education, University of California, Berkeley. We also received very useful suggestions regarding our questionnaire from George Baker, professor of education, University of Texas, Austin.

We are particularly grateful to the chief executive officers of our study institutions: Gary Edelbrock, Allan Hancock College; Ronald Horvath, Jefferson Community College District; Robert McCabe, Miami-Dade Community College; Peter MacDougall, Santa Barbara City College; Richard Moore, Santa Monica College; Jack Randall, Mt. San Antonio College; Peter Spina, Monroe Community College; and Thomas Van Groningen, Yosemite Community College District.

Finally, on a personal level, each of us would like to credit people who simply made room in their lives for us to do this work. We are both grateful for calm, good-natured support from the chancellor's office staff: Catharine Bau-

knight, Jon O'Bergh, and Pamela Smith. Jon O'Bergh gra-
ciously agreed to prepare the index for the book—a complicated assignment which he accomplished with his usual
intelligence and attention to detail. At a critical stage, we
received very helpful comments on an early draft from Cyril
Gulassa, Geraldine Kaspar, Brenda Lovas, and William Pat-
terson. Lovas wishes to thank his sons Timothy, Gregory,
and Desmond for tolerating his absence; his parents, Frank
and Ann, for creating his presence; and his wife, Brenda,
whose generous spirit and ready wit sustain his life. Fryer
wishes to thank Peggy for her abiding love, reliable advice,
and steady good humor; Ray, Gerry, Al, Bob, and Mickey for
their support and inspiration; and Bill J. Priest, Reed L. Buf-
fington, and Peter Masiko, Jr., who gave him his start in this
work and taught him a great deal.

December 1989   Thomas W. Fryer, Jr.
                                        Mountain View, California

                                        John C. Lovas
                                        Palo Alto, California

The Authors

Thomas W. Fryer, Jr., has been chancellor and district superintendent of the Foothill-De Anza Community College District, California, since 1978. He is also visiting professor in
the Graduate School of Education at the University of California, Berkeley. He received his B.A. degree (1958) from
Wayland College in English, his M.A. degree (1959) from Van-
derbilt University in English, and his Ph.D. degree (1968)
from the University of California, Berkeley, in higher education. Fryer began his career in education as an instructor of
English at Daytona Beach Junior College in 1959. He served
as chancellor of the Peralta Colleges in Oakland, California
(1973-1978), and was founding campus chief executive of the
Wolfson Campus of Miami-Dade Community College (1967-
1973). He held the post of assistant dean of instruction for
evening and extension operations at Chabot College, Hay-
ward, California (1965-1967), and was administrative intern
and assistant to the president at American River College,
Sacramento, California (1962-1964).

Fryer has served as a member of the board of directors
of the American Council on Education and of the American
Association for Higher Education. He has been president of
the Florida Association of Community Colleges, president of
the Chief Executive Officers of California Community Colleges, chairperson of the Western Association of Schools and
Colleges Accrediting Commission for Community and Junior
Colleges, and president of the Board of Directors of the
League for Innovation in the Community College. He is the
founder of the National Effective Transfer Consortium.

In 1978, Fryer was named by the editors of *Change* mag-
azine and the American Council on Education as one of 100

young leaders of the academy; in 1986, he was designated one of the most effective college presidents in the nation by an Exxon Education Foundation national study; and, in 1989, he was named one of the nation's top 50 community college chief executives in a national study conducted at the University of Texas, Austin.

Fryer is the author of numerous articles and chapters in edited volumes, and he is a frequent speaker on leadership, governance, and teaching and learning.

John C. Lovas has been a member of the English faculty of De Anza College since 1977; from 1965 to 1977 he served on the English faculty of Foothill College. Lovas received his B.A. degree (1960) from John Carroll University in English and his M.A. degree (1965) from the University of Utah in English and linguistics. He has completed all requirements but the dissertation in a doctoral program at the Stanford University School of Education.

Lovas's interest in leadership began when he served as editor of his campus newspaper, *The Carroll News.* His first experience with organizational decision making and communication came when, as a twenty-two-year-old second lieutenant, he was assigned to run the U.S. Army officers' club in Bremerhaven, Germany. Since then, Lovas has served in a wide range of roles, including assistant division chair at Foothill College; division dean at De Anza College; codirector of multicultural programs for the Foothill-De Anza district; president of AFT Local 1676; president of the Administrative Management Association; chief negotiator for the Certificated Employees Council (twice); and chair of the Constituting Meeting of the Faculty Association.

Lovas is coauthor of "A New Partnership in Governance" (1986, with J. Coffey), a position paper developed by the California Community College Trustee and CEO Task Force on Governance; this document played a significant role in the reform movement of California community colleges in the 1980s. He has published a number of articles on the teaching of writing. In 1979, he participated in a National Endowment for the Humanities seminar at the University of Southern California. In 1989, he served as a Josephine Miles Fellow at the University of California, Berkeley.

Part One

The Nature and Function
of Leadership in
Governance

Chapter One

How Leadership and Governing Structures Shape Decision-Making Climates

*"He that goeth about to persuade a multitude
that they are not so well governed as they ought to be
shall never want attentive and favorable hearers."*
—Richard Hooker

Defining Leadership

This book shows how leaders can direct the power of decision making to serve institutional purposes, a concept we call leadership in governance. Over twenty-five years ago, Vance Packard defined leadership as "the art of getting others to want to do something that you are convinced should be done" (1962, p. 170). Kouzes and Posner adopted this definition in 1987 in their book *The Leadership Challenge.* John Gardner defines leadership as "the process of persuasion and example by which an individual (or leadership team) induces a group to take action that is in accord with the leader's purpose or the shared purposes of all" (1986, p. 45). James MacGregor Burns, in his Pulitzer Prize–winning book *Leadership,* defines the concept as "leaders inducing followers to act for certain goals that represent the values and the motivations—the wants and needs, the aspirations and expectations—*of both leaders and followers*" (1978, p. 28).

For our purposes here, we define leadership as the art of getting others to want to do something that leaders are convinced should be done in service of the institution's mis-

3

sion. There are many other important meanings for the word that we do not address here, and we do not imply that *leadership* in its many forms and contexts is limited to our present definition.

Three aspects of this definition attract us. First, leadership is an art. This means that leadership is complex, not simple. Leadership does not yield its deepest meanings to quick and superficial examination. Practitioners searching for fast, formulaic answers are not likely to find them. It may be possible to be a one-minute manager; it is not possible to be a one-minute leader. The paradox and complexity of community college leadership form a major theme of this work. We recognize the wisdom of the admonition: Do not say I have found the truth. Say, I have found a truth. We accept Niels Bohr's concept of paradox when he says, "The opposite of a small truth is obviously false. The opposite of a great truth is also true."

The complex issues of leadership and governance in institutions have received considerable treatment in the literature, yet a great deal is not known about these important subjects. Seasoned practitioners, who have learned much from their years of experience, are particularly vulnerable to the belief that they understand how leadership and decision making work in their institutions. They are, of course, both right and wrong. Leaders are learners. The study that led to the preparation of this book has strengthened our belief in the limitations of our present understanding. Much as we do know, there is much more to learn, and as with art, new forms and new ways of knowing constantly emerge.

Second, the essence of this definition is in getting others *to want* to do something that leaders believe is important. For us that something is service to the highest sense of institutional purpose. Kouzes and Posner suggest that the clearest distinction between management and leadership is in the difference between getting others to do and getting others to want to do. "Managers," they say, "get other people to do, but leaders get other people to want to do" (1987, p. 27). For leadership to exist, therefore, there must be followers, persons

who have chosen—volunteered—to do something they are not
required to do, and who have undertaken this voluntary activity because they want to do it. This is a rigorous conception.
It means that there may be persons in high places—presidents,
deans, chancellors, trustees—who are not leaders at all, while
others in the same institutions—secretaries, faculty members,
custodians—may exercise significant leadership. Thus, our
definition holds that leadership is plural, that institutions
often have more than one leader, that usually there are multiple leaders operating at many levels and among many institutional constituencies.

The best organizations value both management and
leadership. A. Bartlett Giamatti, the late president of Yale
University, implicitly acknowledges this in his essay "The
Academic Mission":

> American institutions . . . for higher education . . . are not perceived as leading, . . . because, in fact, the institutions themselves, while
> being competently managed in most cases, are
> not necessarily themselves being led.
>
> Management is the capacity to handle multiple problems, neutralize various constituencies,
> motivate personnel. . . . Leadership, on the other
> hand, is an essentially moral act, not—as in most
> management—an essentially protective act. It is
> the assertion of a vision, not simply the exercise
> of a style: the moral courage to assert a vision of
> the institution in the future and the intellectual
> energy to persuade the community or the culture
> of the wisdom and validity of the vision. It is to
> make the vision practicable, and compelling
> [1988, p. 36].

In our view, successful organizations develop effective leaders
and good managers at all levels.

In fact, as we stated above, institutions almost always
have more leaders than the titular leaders realize. Within the

faculty, the support staff, even the ranks of the administration, there are respected individuals whose counsel is valued by their fellows and who are capable of getting others to want to do something these leaders feel is important. The institution's nominal leadership can ignore these people, it can work against them, or it can provide the kind of leadership that aligns these disparate leaders in service to overarching institutional purposes. We develop this concept of alignment more fully in Chapter Four.

Third, the leadership we are concerned with here is *institutional* leadership. Institutional governance is not an end in itself. It is a means to ensure that organizations achieve their missions as effectively as possible. The audiences we address in this book are made up of all those people—trustees, administrators, faculty, students, community members—who wish to see their institution achieve its maximum potential in the service of its purposes. No one is free, of course, of self-interest or personal motivation. These perfectly legitimate interests are always with us. But in this book we emphasize the institution and leadership that works toward the fundamental good for which the institution exists: providing educational services to students.

Defining Governance

Governance, as we define it, comprises the institution's structures and processes for decision making and the communication related to those structures and processes. Almost every discussion of organizational effectiveness acknowledges the crucial importance of communication. Decision making, on the other hand, is often presented as just one of many important organizational processes, like budgeting, information processing, or coordinating. We claim it is much more than that. By decision making we mean the whole complex of an institution's processes for communicating, planning, deciding, acting, and reacting. Though deciding—the discrete act of an individual or group in an institutional context—permeates all institutional activity, we find it helpful to treat such acts as one aspect of the whole process of decision making. Before any organizational structure is set in place, decisions concerning the nature of this structure have been made. Before communication occurs between individuals or groups in an organization, those individuals or groups must decide to communicate. Before an institution begins to plan, someone or some group makes a decision to plan. At the very heart of institutional functioning lies the distribution of resources—human, financial, and physical. Resources are allocated on the basis of decisions made somewhere by someone.

Our view is that decision-making and communication processes, namely, how decisions are made; who makes them; the time, place, and manner in which they are made; and the communicating related to decisions, essentially determine how well the institution achieves its mission over time.

When a person in the organization has an idea, that person must decide whether to forget it or to try to do something with it. If the latter course is chosen, someone or some group must decide what is to be done with the idea. If the idea is rejected, the originator must decide whether to let it go at that, persist at greater length, or accept W. C. Fields's advice: "If at first you don't succeed, try again. Then quit. No use being a damn fool about it."

Everyone in every community college makes decisions all the time—consciously and unconsciously, deliberately and by indecision. Students are deciding whether to do their homework assignments and whether to turn them in on time. Custodians are deciding just how clean they will get the spaces assigned as their responsibility. Teachers are deciding how they will present a specific unit of subject matter and how much of themselves they will give to the task of reaching all the students in their very heterogeneous classes. Administrators are deciding whether to carry through enthusiastically on projects important to the boss or merely to go through the motions. Registration clerks are deciding how they will treat the people lined up at the window. Secretaries are deciding how they will deal with a person on the phone asking for information that is not readily at hand.

Since such decisions are so ordinary, so commonplace, their importance is often not recognized. Many of these decisions seem automatic; certainly they should not be seen as formal or even informal parts of institutional governance mechanisms. Still, these everyday individual decisions are vital to institutional effectiveness. We believe that institutional governance—the organization's official processes for deciding and communicating—creates conditions and establishes a climate within which these and many other decisions are made. To illustrate, recently we heard from a senior faculty member who was frustrated and demoralized because, after repeated attempts over several years, he has had no success in getting the ancient, tattered blackout curtains in his classroom removed and new ones installed, obtaining a sixteen-millimeter movie projector with a stop-action switch, or having the table in the front of his classroom replaced with a desk. The processes of institutional decision making and communication—governance—had handled, or, depending on one's point of view, mishandled, these requests, and in doing so had created a psychological climate within which this person made many of his decisions concerning his teaching. We believe that to the extent this professor's effectiveness was reduced by his frustration, his service to his institution's mission was also reduced. Furthermore, his appraisal of the value the institution placed on him as an individual and on his teaching was diminished. People who do not believe their institution values them are hindered in valuing their institution.

In another institution, discussions were under way in a planning committee concerning a new technology center that was soon to be built on campus—a state-of-the-art, highly sophisticated facility. One faculty member in the group, when asked his opinion on a matter under discussion, replied, "Some of us faculty have a hard time getting excited about all this high-tech stuff when we can't get the wall outlet in the lecture hall fixed." One of our study institutions was cautioned on this very point in a recent accreditation report:

> Strategic planning has been raised to an unusually high level within the College and that is commendable. Certainly the vision and sights of the College community have been raised. People are looking at opportunities and their roles in new and challenging ways. However, as the attention of the institution becomes focused on Strategic Planning and the lofty strategic goals, sight cannot be lost of the central institutional mission which is to teach, to provide that opportunity for learning. The classroom environment, the teaching-learning environment, must always be a primary concern of the College. Sophisticated and intricate planning processes do not preclude or supersede the need for careful and conscious attention to such mundane but practical issues as classroom sound distractions, HVAC [heating, ventilating, and air conditioning] concerns, and even classroom basics—seating, chalk, screens [Evaluation Team . . . , 1985, p. 11].

The quality of day-to-day life in organizations is created by such small matters, which also establish the basis on which people decide how they are valued by the institution. We believe that in organizations there are correlates to the elements in Maslow's hierarchy of needs. People's basic needs must be met before they can be expected to make higher-order contributions, a principle, we believe, college officials should take pains to understand and master if they wish their institution to achieve its maximum effectiveness.

Leadership in Governance

All faculty and staff are employed to serve the institution's mission. The point at which these individual human beings touch the governance of the enterprise is the nexus where leadership in governance occurs. By *leadership in governance* we mean the creation of conditions, through institutional processes for decision making and communication, under which organizational participants *want* to contribute more than the bare minimum required of them in the service of the institution's purposes and where the many organizational leaders are roughly aligned in service of the institution's mission. We will develop this point in Chapter Four—"Deciding."

The Role of Governance in Creating
Organizational Structures

When a new institution is established, the founders must make innumerable decisions about its basic structure. Categories of employment must be established. In community colleges as in other colleges and universities, these categories almost universally include a chief executive officer who acts on behalf of the board of trustees, and some arrangement of administrators, faculty, and support staff (often called "classified"). Work units are established according to the functions the college must carry out. Academic divisions or departments are created, thereby grouping some faculty together but dividing them from other faculty. Budget categories are defined, thereby identifying how resources will be allocated and how their use will be accounted for.

As these various categories are created, formal relationships among them are defined, most commonly in some form of organizational chart. Such charts illustrate the lines of authority and responsibility among the various departments, functions, and categories of employees. The literature on structure in organizations is rich in discussions of the merits of various frameworks, such as hierarchical, flat, and matrix.

As a college develops, there is usually a parallel increase in the formal definition of functions, roles, and relationships. Job titles are established and connected to a system of pay grades. Responsibilities of such jobs are specified in writing and used both in the process of hiring new people and in evaluating their performance.

As a college grows, some form of a relatively complex, bureaucratic decision structure inevitably is established. Various officers, official groups, committees, councils, forums, senates, and unions are created by the governing board and members of the organization. Such entities often require coordinating, advisory, and recommending bodies. Those who are privileged with membership in these bodies are the organizational members most active in the formal process of institutional governance.

Many of the structural elements of a college are so institutionalized, so much a part of the culture of the institution, that they are no longer distinguished as features of the organizational landscape. They seem to have emerged nearly by genetic action, giving rise, no doubt, to the definition of culture as "everything you know you didn't know you knew." Many members of the organization do not imagine any other way of doing things. Our study of various institutions confirmed this observation. The clear lines drawn between administrators, faculty, and support staff suggest almost a "natural" arrangement and, in some cases, a natural hierarchy. Yet, the differences in how such groups relate in the decision-making processes of various colleges demonstrate that most of these arrangements and hierarchies are not natural at all but are created and maintained by the people of a given college.

We find it useful to remember that a particular structure can create perceptual blinders. In many California community colleges, salary decisions have evolved through four different formats: unilateral board and administrative action, informal "finance" committees involving faculty, "meet and confer" councils defined in state law, and collective bargaining arrangements. Although these structures differ in important ways, in the last three cases we can see that faculty collectively exert some influence on the rate of pay increase and that "naturally" all faculty would receive a uniform rate of increase. In Kentucky, Jefferson Community College does not have collective bargaining; rather, there is a system of merit pay for faculty, with the final decision on pay increases made by the president for each faculty member individually.

The president is guided by a formula that defines the kinds of activities faculty must document to merit increases at various levels, but the increases are not the same for everyone.

Looked at from the perspective of California salary negotiation practices, the structure of the Jefferson system appeared to make no allowance for the faculty collectively to affect the level of compensation awarded each year. But as we talked to more people and gathered more data, we learned that each year a faculty committee reviews the factors in the merit pay formula. Thus, by lobbying through this committee, the faculty as a whole can influence the way in which pay increases are granted. This experience reminded us that function is not inherent in any particular structure, that very different structures may accomplish quite similar functions.

Birnbaum uses the term *bureaucracy* to describe the organizational structure of community colleges. He says, "The word *bureaucracy* is so burdened by connotations of rigidity, waste, and lack of human concern that merely mentioning it in the context of college life almost always provokes responses ranging from helpless shrugs to cries of outrage. A useful discussion of the college as a bureaucracy must therefore begin by using the word in a descriptive and analytical rather than a pejorative sense. . . . We will consider *bureaucracy* to refer to 'the type of organization designed to accomplish large-scale administrative tasks by systematically coordinating the work of many individuals' " (1988, p. 107).

In every community college we know, there are defined organizational structures, described visually in line and staff organizational charts and narratively in written job descriptions. Such charts and position descriptions represent rational efforts to link means to ends, to divide the work of the institution reasonably into assigned duties and responsibilities, and to establish accountability. In the larger community colleges these structures are highly complex. They are further complicated when the campus is part of a larger system containing other campuses. We shall say more on this in Chapter Two.

In most community colleges the structure as displayed in the organization chart is generally known and accepted by the participants as one of the ordinary facts of life. A faculty member would identify himself as a member of the physics department, which is part of the natural sciences division within the office of instruction of the college, which is one of three colleges in a community college district. Without such structures, even with their inherent limitations and sometimes negative side effects, institutions would be much less effective in pursuing their mission. What is almost never charted and published is the institution's structure for decision making, setting forth where, in what groups or by which individuals, at what times and places, under what conditions, in consultation with whom, touching which subjects, employing what information, using what processes, decisions are made. Rarely could a new member of the physics department read a document that would delineate what choices were his alone, which decisions needed departmental review, which would be decided at the division level, when the vice president for instruction or the president would have to be consulted, or when the union, the district chancellor's cabinet, or the board of trustees would need to participate. This knowledge is usually acquired through experience and is never fully acquired by some organizational participants.

Usually the decision-making structure is related to the organizational structure but often in unexpected ways. When a district trustee is lobbied for additional resources by a personal friend who happens to be one of the presidents in a multicollege system, and when that trustee goes to the district's CEO privately demanding special treatment for her friend's campus, if the CEO acquiesces, the resulting decision is clearly related to the organization chart but in ways that have more to do with power, politics, and personality than with rationality and structure. We now turn to these less rational aspects of institutional governance.

The Role of Personality in Governance and in Creating Organizational Climate

When a dean decides how to respond to requests from two department chairpersons, only one of whom the dean likes personally, she makes a governance decision. When a business manager decides how to deal with the news he has just received that the adopted budget for the college district contains a major error in budgeted revenue, he makes a governance decision.

Such situations, the decisions made as a result of them, the time, place, and manner in which these decisions are made, along with thousands of other situations and the decisions that flow out of them, literally create the institution—its character, its climate, and its effectiveness. As we have said, decision making is not just another institutional activity, a kind of impersonalized abstraction like *planning*. For better or worse, decision making is hard-wired into the institution's central nervous and motor systems.

In community college governance, the personalities of the key players—trustees, administrators, faculty, staff, and in some cases student leaders—interact with the organizational structures and processes in ways that help create an institution's environment or climate. *Climate*, as we use the term here, is the ambient, affective character of a place—the conditions that evoke feelings, either positive or negative, from the people in the organization. Climate is to the affective aspect of human beings in an organization what air is to the physical aspect. Climate is an organization's emotional atmosphere. People breathe it. The circumstances under which all the people in the organization do their work establish the quality of this climate, evoking commitment or apathy, enthusiasm or cynicism, positive energy or negative energy. Because the structures and processes for decision making and communication help control the institutional climate of a community college, we see governance as a critical vehicle for exercising leadership.

Recent opinion research conducted in the workplace, while not specifically using the term *climate*, seems to validate our interpretation that decision making and its affective consequences are enormously important. Writing in the September 1988 *Training and Development Journal*, Patricia Galagan cites a Daniel Yankelovich study (1988) that suggests that while U.S. workers like their jobs, they generally do not like their companies as places to work, and in many cases they do not work as hard as they could. A Gallup poll asked employees if they would work harder and do a better job if they were more involved in *decisions* relating to their work (emphasis added). Eighty-four percent said they would. Yankelovich feels that it is the leaders who run our institutions that do not understand the people who work for them: "tens of millions of well-educated Americans, proud of their achievements, zealous of their freedoms, motivated by new values, with substantial control over their own production, and ready to raise their level of effort if given the proper encouragement" (Galagan, 1988, p. 37).

Decision making is not only very powerful, but because it is done by human beings, it is also very personal, whether carried out by institutional officials in the discharge of their official responsibilities or undertaken by rank and file employees of the enterprise. Key decision makers include everyone with managerial or supervisory responsibility in the organization: presidents, deans, directors, coordinators, and the like. They also include everyone who heads a constituency or has a following—for example, a union president or an esteemed faculty person or a classified staff member whose opinions are listened to and respected by his or her colleagues.

To illustrate using our previous example: The business manager upon learning of the error in budgeted revenues decides to take this news directly to his president. The president then hears for the first time that the funds available to her college are quite different from the figures in the published budget. She must now decide how to deal with that information: act on it unilaterally or in consultation with her business manager, disclose it to others and discuss it, withhold it, or do something else. When the information, sooner or later, finds its way to the union, the union president must decide when and how to communicate to both the union leadership and the union membership. This decision is also a very powerful one, and it is often determined, in large part, by the president's candor and timeliness of disclosure.

Because we see governance as a complicated matter involving both structures and persons, we use the term, much as Birnbaum does, "in a very broad way to refer to the structures and processes through which institutional participants interact with and influence each other and communicate with the larger environment" (1988, p. 4). By *structures* we also include the absence of structure, as when a decision is made unilaterally, in isolation and without consultation, by a person in a position of influence or organizational authority.

What we mean by our last point can be illustrated by an unusual incident in one of our interviews. The leader of a staff organization, who was personally at odds with most of the college leadership (and in fact was under challenge as leader of her own organization), announced at the outset of her interview that she would leave promptly at 4:30 P.M. because that was when the contract said her workday ended and no overtime had been authorized for this activity. Throughout the interview, her responses were hostile and sarcastic. Such behavior by an individual in a leadership role has an impact on governance, not the least of which is that other leaders must deal with the consequences of the behavior, often devoting disproportionate amounts of time and energy to mollifying the individual, explaining her idiosyncrasies to others, or dealing with the aftermath of her actions among those organizational members who follow her lead.

Individual people interact with organizational structures and processes in other ways. For example, many people in the institution want to have a sense of pride in their boss. Peters and Waterman (1982) concluded from their search for excellent companies that the people in them wanted a sense of positive reinforcement, a sense of pride from their work. They wanted to feel they were winners and part of a winning team. We are aware of a secretary who said to her boss as he was on his way out of the office to give a speech, "Make us proud!" We believe that most people want to be proud of their work, their workplace, and their leaders. Kouzes and Posner (1987) found that people want leaders who are honest, competent, forward-looking, and inspiring. These are qualities that workers can be proud of, and it behooves persons in positions of authority to think about what they do and do not do that would create or destroy such pride.

Clearly, decision making involves the exercise of choice as an act of official organizational authority, but it can also involve the interpersonal behavior of persons in formal or informal positions of power in the organization. Such aspects of management style as *wandering around* and *huddling* recognize the importance of these less formal contacts among members of the organization. Richard Moore, president of Santa Monica College, has such a distinctive personal style that faculty and staff know that when he walks through campus he can be approached with ideas, and that when he wants informal input on an idea or prospective decision, he approaches the concerned person and suggests they "take a walk." Even the exercise of personal discretion in matters of professional friendships and social networks can take on some of the character of official authority within the organization. Some years ago a faculty leader we know asserted that an administrator in his institution cultivated personal relationships with staff members, took an interest in their family situations, sought out opportunities for social interaction, and showed an interest in personal gossip about individuals as a way to gain leverage on them in their employment situations. Demonstrating sensitivity to this issue and wishing not to misuse social relationships, a seasoned board member at Santa Barbara City College noted that, in a small town, social contact between the board and faculty inevitably occurs. "We are friendly—we are discreet," she commented.

Little discussion of this interpersonal dimension of governance is found in the literature. Everyone would agree that the final decision by a college president to recommend a particular candidate to the governing board for appointment as a new vice president is a governance decision. But we go further: In a committee meeting, when a dean berates a committee member who has raised an awkward question that the dean did not wish raised, she has also made a governance decision. When an academic division chair arranges a more

desirable teaching schedule for a faculty member who supports the chair than he is willing to arrange for the division
critic who shows the chair no support whatever, yet another
governance decision has been made, one that contributes to
creating the environment in the division. These cases illustrate the way in which decisions are made. When, where, and
how decisions are made—whether through formally established structures and processes, or informal, interpersonal relationships—matters a great deal because each act of deciding
contributes to the creation of the organization's climate.

Since we believe the interpersonal behavior of people
in positions of power or influence constitutes an important
aspect of institutional governance, we want to say more about
the role of personalities in institutional affairs. By *personalities* we mean simply the people who form the cast of characters in the organization. We use the term as a convenient way
to refer to the unique mix of individuals in an organization
at a given time. Even though we claim that institutional governance is a personality-sensitive matter, it is paradoxical that,
in one sense, personalities make no difference at all. When
today's CEO leaves, tomorrow's CEO takes his or her place.
In that structural sense, who or what the CEO is matters very
little. At the same time, both the day-to-day quality of life for
institutional participants and the overall character of the institution's environment are highly sensitive to the interpersonal
behavior of key players, particularly persons in positions of
institutional authority. Thus, personalities at once make no
difference and make all the difference.

We believe that the role of personalities in governance
varies both among and within institutional types. One
hundred fifty years ago Emerson claimed that "an institution
is the lengthened shadow of one man." We find this idea
overly simple and misleading, but careful observers with
extended service in organizations also know that the statement
contains elements of truth. How does the influence of one
individual cast a shadow over organizational functioning?
Here is one way. Members of the administrative staff tend to
be responsive to the wishes of their superiors. In administra-

tions, many subordinates deliberately behave in ways they know to be desired by the person at the top, or at least in ways they know will be approved by that person. In some cases where middle managers have a complex decision to make, they consciously ask themselves, "What would the boss do in this situation?" Thus, over time, as individuals in the administrative hierarchy act in ways they know are desired or approved by the CEO, the institution's culture takes on some of the characteristics of that person. To illustrate, anonymous responses in an evaluation of a presentation on governance at one of the study institutions identified as "most useful" the "opinions of the chancellor and the president—those are the ones that funnel down."

In extreme forms, when what funnels down is highly directive, requiring unquestioning compliance, the effect on the human spirit can be profound, as Vaclav Havel, writer and later president of Czechoslovakia, makes plain in a 1975 open letter to the general secretary of the Czechoslovak Communist Party:

> If every day a man takes orders in silence from an incompetent superior, if every day he solemnly performs ritual acts which he privately finds ridiculous, if he unhesitatingly gives answers to questionnaires which are contrary to his real opinions and is prepared to deny his own self in public, if he sees no difficulty in feigning sympathy or even affection where, in fact, he feels only indifference or aversion, it still does not mean that he has entirely lost the use of one of the basic human senses, namely, the sense of *humiliation*.
>
> On the contrary: even if they never speak of it, people have a very acute appreciation of the price they have paid for outward peace and quiet: the permanent *humiliation of their human dignity*. The less direct resistance they put up to it— comforting themselves by driving it from their mind and deceiving themselves with the thought

that it is of no account, or else simply gritting their teeth—the deeper the experience etches itself into their emotional memory. The man who can resist humiliation can quickly forget it; but the man who can long tolerate it must long remember it. In actual fact, then, nothing remains forgotten. All the fear one has endured, the dissimulation one has been forced into, all the painful and degrading buffoonery, and, worst of all, perhaps, the feeling of displayed cowardice—all this settles and accumulates somewhere on the bottom of our social consciousness, quietly fermenting [1986, p. 31].

The effect on the institution of the personality at the top depends as well on the nature of the institution. As we shall see in Chapter Four, Birnbaum borrows Cohen and March's (1974) concept of "organized anarchy" in sketching his portrait of a major research university. He contrasts this institution with People's Community College, a bureaucracy where a rational division of labor and a hierarchy of authority attempt to link means to ends. Hierarchical relationships are characteristic of bureaucracies, and at People's a good deal of power is exercised at the top by the president. By power we mean the capacity to make things happen in the organization, to get things done. In institutions where significant power is wielded by the CEO, the personality of that individual becomes more important than in institutions where this is not the case. The issue for governance is to ensure that individual leaders do not assume greater importance than institutional purposes. When personality overwhelms purpose the organization as a whole suffers.

Even in institutions where power is exercised through a bureaucracy, however, gauging the effect that particular individuals have on decision making is difficult. Since presidents are usually selected to reflect the values of their institutions, presidents themselves may become the "lengthened shadow" of the organization rather than the other way around. Further complicating the effects of individuals on institutions, the absence of leadership is often difficult to observe. Leadership almost always involves initiating and usually requires risk taking. Most participants simply observe actions that are initiated, not those that are not. Thus, many organizations seem to get along quite well without leadership. Since participants see only what happens—not what does not—and as long as conditions are generally satisfactory in the institution, few people realize that leadership could make a difference.

Our definition of leadership, the art of getting people to want to contribute more than they are required to in the service of institutional purposes, imposes a higher standard than simply being good. Many perfectly fine institutions operate with almost everyone doing roughly what is expected, little more, little less. Defining, diagnosing, and closing the gap between adequate and excellent, between compliance and commitment, is not an easy task, and many individuals, many institutions, and many departments within institutions simply lack the will to make the major effort required to achieve incremental improvements. When being good is good enough or when an organization begins to coast, leadership becomes "dispensable" (Selznick, 1957), and caretaker administrations may serve usefully. Under such conditions the effects of individuals may diminish.

So personalities matter, but differently in different organizational cultures and under different circumstances. To argue that personalities make no difference in institutions is to argue that any similar group of thirty-five men meeting in Philadelphia in the summer of 1787 would have produced a comparable result. Undoubtedly there are those who would argue just that. We believe otherwise. We believe that the fortuitous combination of circumstance and personality can produce unique results, for good or ill, and changes in the mix would yield results of a materially different character.

We have tried to show that governance, the structures and processes for institutional decision making and communication, is a critical and underused vehicle for the exercise of leadership and that in organizations the interaction of structure and personality helps create the climate for decision making. But all these elements of governance operate in a larger frame. An organization's historical and administrative context conditions these interactions in complex, subtle ways. Thus, before we examine how leadership can be exercised through governance in community colleges, we must consider the important elements of context in which all community colleges find themselves.

Chapter Highlights

- Leadership, for our purposes, is the art of getting others to want to do something that leaders are convinced should be done in service to the institution's mission.

- The paradox and complexity of community college governance form a major theme of this work.

- Governance, as we define it, comprises the institution's structures and processes for decision making and communication.

- Decision making is an enormously powerful activity, one that determines how well the institution achieves its mission over time.

- Everyone in every community college makes decisions all the time—consciously and unconsciously, deliberately and by indecision—and these everyday decisions are much more important than is commonly understood.

- Institutional governance creates conditions within which thousands of small, unconscious, everyday decisions are made.

- By *leadership in governance* we mean the creation of climates under which organizational participants want to contribute more than the bare minimum required of them in service to the institution's purpose.

- *Climate,* as we use the term, is an organization's emotional atmosphere.

- Decision making at every level is an enormously powerful activity, hard-wired into the institution's central nervous and motor systems.

• The personalities of key individuals—trustees, administrators, faculty, staff, and in some cases student leaders—interact with the organizational structures and processes in ways that help create an institution's climate.

• Decision making is not only very powerful but also very personal, whether carried out by institutional officials or undertaken by rank and file employees of the enterprise.

• The overall quality of the institutional environment is highly sensitive to the interpersonal behavior of key figures, particularly, but not exclusively, persons in positions of organizational authority.

• The idea of an organization as the "lengthened shadow" of the person at the top is both misleading and useful in thinking about the role of officials in an organization.

• Individuals matter in organizational destinies but in complicated ways, and differently in different organizational cultures and under different circumstances.

• Since leading almost always involves initiating and usually requires risk taking, its absence is often not easily observed.

• Leadership may become dispensable where there is no aspiration for excellence or during periods of organizational quiescence.

Chapter Two

The Context for Decision Making in the Community College

"Fellow citizens, we cannot escape history."
—Abraham Lincoln

"A community is like a ship;
everyone ought to be prepared to take the helm."
—Henrik Ibsen

"A man may love a paradox
without either losing his wit or his honesty."
—Ralph Waldo Emerson

So far we have tried to elaborate the conceptual frame of our work, delineating the interrelationships of leadership, governance, structure, climate, and personality. But these concepts do not operate in a vacuum. Decision-making processes in community colleges occur in particular contexts. Before we focus on specific contextual aspects of deciding in Chapter Four, we want to suggest some of the major forces that have shaped the community colleges in which people decide. Those forces include almost ninety years of history, the uniquely local character of the colleges, the emergence of large community college systems, both in local communities and in states, and such twentieth-century American cultural values as materialism, efficiency, and technology. In this chapter, we also discuss the contextual issues that led to the research project that influenced the preparation of this book.

The Role of History in Shaping Institutional Character

Community colleges, viewed from the traditional models of secondary and higher education, are structurally and conceptually ambiguous institutions. Their local governing boards and extensive community root systems are vestiges of their high school histories. The fact that they offer the full, two-year lower-division component of baccalaureate degree programs places them squarely in the domain of higher education. This conceptual ambiguity is further reflected in a certain inherent tension in the institution's governance. In the historical secondary model, decision making was largely a top-down activity, beginning at the top with the school board and carried out internally by the board's administrative staff. The university model, in contrast, assigns administration a first-among-equals role, with faculty dominating decision making in many key areas. The tensions between these models characterize community colleges.

In the early decades of this century, junior colleges were created from equal parts of the university moving down and the high school moving up. Around the turn of the century, several prominent university presidents proposed that the first two years of undergraduate study, the years that completed students' general education, be severed from the university and be provided in what President William Rainey Harper of the University of Chicago was the first to call a "junior college." Walter Crosby Eells, writing about the curriculum of this new institution, cites a 1929 University of Chicago conference that articulates the paradox: "It is the final institution to deal with general education, and it is also under obligation to use the last stages of general education in preparing the student to undertake critical, independent thinking. The student should pass out of the junior college matured by his training to the point where he is ready to enter the field of constructive thinking" (1931, p. 475).

During this same period it was becoming apparent to leaders of American industry, agriculture, and business that young people needed more extensive technical and vocational preparation for work than could be provided in the high school. Thus, junior colleges became at once lower-division preparation for advanced undergraduate work at the university and post-high school training for occupations in business, industry, and agriculture.

Following World War II, most junior colleges became "open-door" institutions. No other development has more powerfully influenced their character. The open door ordained that the institution would be distinctively local, shaped by the ethnicity, gender, age, and income levels of the students who came through the door. In California, this meant that eligible students were defined as high school graduates or those eighteen years of age or over "who are capable of profiting from instruction" (California Education Code, Sec. 76000). As Glen Bushnell, a De Anza College counselor, puts it: "At De Anza, we take in the top 100 per cent of the high school graduates." Or, as Fred Shaw, a former University of Miami faculty member who joined the staff of Miami-Dade Junior College in its early years, described college admissions: "At Dade Junior we've got the toughest admissions requirement of any college in the country. You've got to be able to make a left turn off 27th Avenue into the campus." Such policies meant that junior colleges became and have remained market-sensitive institutions, highly responsive to the needs and interests of their students and their local communities. Thus, when the ranks of those attending college expanded from primarily the children of the privileged to all "who are capable of profiting from instruction," the proportion of first-generation college students grew significantly, creating a demand for extensive counseling and advisement services. When more and more students with spotty or inadequate academic preparation entered, the colleges developed increasingly extensive remedial programs. When women began entering the work force in dramatically larger numbers, community colleges created "re-entry" programs. When the economy produced extended leisure time for adults, many of them turned to their local colleges for further general education, education in the arts, and programs in civic awareness,

recreation, and avocational pursuits, thus giving impetus
to "community service" programs. As communities, working with their colleges, identified the needs of ethnic minor-
ities or recent immigrants and refugees, multicultural and
bilingual programs and curricula in English as a second
language were established. And on and on it goes. Quickly
responding to community and student needs, the colleges'
educational programs have become a mirror image of the
complexity and diversity of the local communities and the
larger society they serve.

Because most community colleges do not maintain selective admission practices, the demographic makeup of the community becomes a critical factor in decisions on curriculum,
on the composition of the faculty, and on resource allocations
of varying kinds. Colleges and universities with selective
admission policies serve regions or the nation at large rather
than a particular community. These institutions can generally
shape the demographics of their student body through admissions policies whereas the demographics of a community college are usually shaped by the particular character of the
communities served by the college. Most of these patterns are
determined by social, political, and economic forces beyond
the control of the college.

Mission, Purpose, and Function

Whether stated formally in writing, articulated informally in
conversations, or simply understood implicitly, the mission
and philosophy of a community college shape the context for
decision making. When members of the organization share
compatible philosophies and hold clear understandings of
institutional mission, decisions are more readily arrived at
than in places where fundamental differences about philosophy and conflicting understandings of mission exist among
leaders and others in the organization. This does not suggest
that diversity should not be valued. A vital college community
engages in continuous dialogue concerning the issues of philosophy and purpose, mission and function. Giamatti put it

this way: "It is that civil conversation—tough, open, principled—between and among all members and parts of the institution that must be preserved. If it is, a community is patiently built" (1988, p. 45).

As junior colleges evolved into community colleges, the accumulation of functions that characterized the change became the source of much confusion about the nature of the institution, both within and outside of the colleges. This confusion is reflected in such phrases as "permanent mission blur," "identity crisis," and "misguided effort to be all things to all people." In fact, community colleges are highly complex institutions. They do not serve a single function; they serve multiple functions. All these real and legitimate functions have made it enormously difficult to articulate what Peter Drucker calls "the clear, simple, penetrating theory" of an institution (1974, p. 74), or what we like to call the "animating idea" of the community college. Where once the mission of the junior college might have been limited to preparing high school graduates for upper-division collegiate work or for technical and business employment, today key elements of the mission are teaching and learning, responding to the emerging educational needs of the community, and helping build community among the people served by the college. The ongoing effort to define mission must avoid the confining effects of a single, simplistic formula while seeking to find a vocabulary that truly expresses the penetrating theory, the animating idea behind the purposes of the community college.

The importance for decision-making contexts is simply this: each of the basic functions of community colleges can call on institutional resources. Since there are no absolute certainties about the interrelationships and relative importance of those functions, program development decisions, resource allocation decisions, and hiring decisions are all made more complicated. The paradox of this eclecticism of mission, however, is that it is also the institution's genius. By avoiding the limiting effects of a narrow, fixed definition, community colleges have been free to serve many of the most

important educational needs of American society over the
past half century.

The Role of Systems

Community colleges grew rapidly during the 1950s and 1960s,
both in enrollment and in numbers of institutions. There
was a time during this period when community colleges were
being established across the country at the rate of about one
per week. In the larger metropolitan areas, institutions that
had begun operations as single campuses began to add new
campus operations. Miami-Dade Community College was
founded in 1960 and began operations on the college's North
Campus. The South Campus was established in 1967; what is
now called the Wolfson Campus was born as the Downtown
Campus in 1971. Miami-Dade is a *multicampus* system. The
institution is headed by a president, and each campus CEO
carries the title of vice president. The Community College of
St. Louis was created in 1963 with three campuses beginning
operation simultaneously: Florissant Valley, Forest Park, and
Meramec. St. Louis is a *multicollege* system. The district is
headed by a chancellor and each college CEO is a president.
Governance is enormously more complicated in institutions
that are parts of local systems. District- or system-level governance is separate from but closely related to campus- or col-
lege-level governance. Certain key players are inevitably
involved in both, increasing the time commitments required
of them. Complex issues involving the locus of decision making and the relationship of the center to the periphery, including agreeing on what is central and what is peripheral, are
crucial to the effective functioning of multiunit community
college systems.

Also during the 1950s and 1960s, state system organizations emerged both to give state-level policy makers clearer
lines of accountability and to give people in the local institutions a sense that someone was speaking for them in state
capitols. Prior to this time, many states had organized community colleges as units within departments of education hav-

ing responsibility for public schools. In Illinois the state board for community colleges was created in 1965; in California, 1967; in North Carolina, 1963. In Florida, a community college unit within the state department of education was set up in the 1950s, but it was not until 1983 that a state board for community colleges was formed. In most situations, state-level bodies, including legislatures, exercise some degree of supervisory and regulatory authority over the local institutions, establishing a context within which local institutional governance operates. Other organizational patterns exist. In Kentucky and Hawaii, for example, community colleges operate as units within the state university. The operation of state-level systems as well as of local systems introduces immense new complications into institutional governance and forms the contextual backdrop against which colleges are governed.

Twentieth-Century Cultural Values

To borrow the title of rock music star Bruce Springsteen's hit song, the community college was "born in the USA" in this century. Not surprisingly, it reflects many values of the society that created it. The materialistic aspirations of the culture, derived from both Calvinist tradition and the ambition of immigrants, have always characterized community college programs. American industry's increasing concern with efficiency and the American polity's concern with equity have been built into the value structure of community colleges. Community colleges grew up with modern technology and are uniquely designed to provide the trained work force demanded by an automobile-driven, computer-based, television-shaped culture.

Despite the limits inherent in an institution reflecting these values, the community college has worked remarkably well in a nation that has undergone profound transformations since World War II. People who work in community colleges tend to take a somewhat simplistic view of their prosperity, thinking they have succeeded because they are simply good people doing good things. A more comprehensive analysis, however, suggests a number of reasons for their successes:

1. Community colleges are convenient. Americans are convenience-seeking people.

2. Community colleges are cheaper. They enjoy a price advantage over the competition.

3. Community colleges have served an incredible population boom. A rising tide lifts all ships.

4. Community colleges have served the interests of universities. They allowed the universities to enjoy the benefits of growth while retaining academic exclusivity.

5. Community colleges serve the social and economic need to elongate adolescence by keeping large numbers of youth out of the labor market for two more years, at the same time providing the technical training now demanded by the workplace.

6. Community colleges serve important social needs growing out of the new awareness and sensitivity to the diversity of America, specifically the civil rights movement, the women's movement, the senior citizen's movement, and the barrier-free society movement.

7. Community colleges provide initial training for occupations as well as retraining for the previously educated, the so-called reverse transfer student, the one with a bachelor's degree and no job who needs new skills to gain employment. Community colleges also provide substantial intellectual fare for local people interested in the continued life of their minds.

8. Community colleges have been responsive, in the words of Cohen and Brawer (1982, p. 4), because they "had no traditions to defend, no alumni to question their role, no autonomous professional staff to be moved aside, and no statements of philosophy that would militate against their taking on responsibility for everything."

In summary, community colleges are conceptually complex organizations that operate in the powerful contexts of institutional history, social values, and unique local communities. Within the institutions every person is a decision maker, a fact that creates an enormous fund of power. Governance is one of the factors that create the conditions within which people decide. The function of leadership in governance is to create the conditions within which people want to decide and want to act in ways that maximize the institution's achievement of its purposes. Leaders achieve this aim most effectively when they bring people into the governance of the institution and make them full partners in its processes. Many fine institutions behave otherwise, but we believe that institutions move toward the fullest achievement of their potential when they consciously grant their members power, creating the conditions under which more of their members want to do more for the institution. We found much evidence of this in our research in the nine community college districts we surveyed. Although we deliberately chose not to write a technical monograph, some contextual material regarding our research should be useful.

The Context of Our Study

The research we draw on in this book was precipitated in quite a particular way. In the mid-1980s, much public criticism and controversy focused on community colleges and on the management of California community colleges in particular. Two or three of the state's seventy districts received a great deal of publicity for alleged mismanagement. The state's Committee on Governmental Efficiency (the so-called Little Hoover Commission) was probing the governance system. And the Commission on the Review of the Master Plan for Higher Education had proposed a radical change in the form of governing community colleges. Understandably, this stream of criticism and negative publicity commanded the attention of community college leaders.

At the spring 1986 meeting of California's statewide Academic Senate, Thomas Fryer asked a group of faculty, administrative, and trustee leaders whether they knew of community college districts that were well run. To the surprise of many, about half of those present (perhaps twenty-five individuals) raised their hands. As Fryer observed at the time:

"Some of us felt that a more useful, constructive approach than the constant barrage of criticism would be to identify situations where local governance was working well, look at what was going on, and try to describe several models of good practice."

In August of that year, we met with the leaders of the trustees' organization, the chief executive officers' organization, and the statewide academic senate. They agreed to cosponsor a study that would be funded and carried out by the Foothill-De Anza Community College District. This original group became the core of an advisory board that included representatives from the California Community College Trustees; the Chief Executive Officers, the Academic Senate, and the Faculty Association of the California Community Colleges; and the Western Association of Schools and Colleges Accrediting Commission for Community and Junior Colleges. Three researchers—one from a community college, one from a state university, and one from a private research firm—also served on the advisory board. These extraordinarily helpful individuals are acknowledged in the Preface.

As our work progressed, we focused principally on internal decision making and communication at the district level but below the level of the governing board. The governing board's role in institutional governance is, to be sure, enormously important. The board creates the environment within which staff members at every level and in every assignment perform their duties. We acknowledge the key role of the governing board and comment on it in Chapter Four. We also became aware in the early stages of our work of the immense complexity that arises in the multiunit community college from the interaction of district-level governance mechanisms both with the state and with campus-level governance.

The initial focus of the study was California. As a first step, we decided to ask all seventy (now seventy-one) community college districts in the state to nominate themselves for participation in the study. Self-nomination required that the district's CEO, its academic senate president, and the president of the board of trustees *jointly* sign this statement:

We recognize that no human organization is perfect or problem free and certainly no community college district is free of conflicts over decision making, communication, resource allocation, policy making, and policy implementation. Yet we believe that in our district our governance process is working effectively, and we wish to be considered as a possible model in the joint study of local governance.

Remarkably, twenty-three districts, approximately one-third of the state total, completed this form. Limited resources made it impossible to examine so large a group of institutions, so a preliminary investigation was undertaken to identify a smaller number of districts with effective governance arrangements to participate in an in-depth study.

This pre-study consisted of a mail survey administered to members of key groups involved in institutional governance as designated by the districts themselves. Five hundred eighty-six questionnaires were mailed to individuals in twenty-one districts (two districts elected not to participate at this point) and 414, over 70 percent, were returned. The eighty-plus-item questionnaire asked respondents to (a) identify the "issues, problems, or challenges" they felt their district had experienced over the last several years; (b) indicate how successfully they felt these issues had been dealt with; and (c) indicate the role district-level governance had played in dealing with the issues. Each item called for responses on a five-point scale, allowing also for nonresponses. (These questionnaires are included in Resource B.) This procedure allowed us to construct tables that reflected average responses for institutions as well as average responses for governance elements within institutions. All these tabulated data were presented to the study advisory board in a coded, comparative format that prevented committee members from identifying individual districts. The district identities were so well masked that one committee member unknowingly used the data to argue against including his own institution. Reviewing the survey data against previously established criteria, the advisory board selected six districts for in-depth study.

In making this selection, board members looked for districts that reported high levels of success in dealing with the issues they faced and indicated as well a strong role for district governance in addressing these issues. In addition, the board took note of the consistency of responses across the constituent groups. For example, the board looked for a high degree of consistency between faculty and administration in the levels of success each reported. The board also considered each district's overall rate of response to the survey and the total number of respondents in each of three critical categories: faculty, administrators, and trustees. The following institutions, each scoring strongly on five of the six criteria, were selected: Allan Hancock College, Santa Maria; Foothill-De Anza Community College District, Los Altos Hills; Mt. San Antonio College, Walnut; Santa Barbara City College, Santa Barbara; Santa Monica College, Santa Monica; and Yosemite Community College District, Modesto (see Institutional Profiles in Resource A.) Though each of these districts enjoys a good reputation, we do not claim they were, or are, the best. Several outstanding California districts chose not to participate.

Again working with the advisory board, we developed a research design that would document each district's internal governance system and corroborate the survey findings that governance played an important role in the district's apparently effective decision-making processes. Using an interview protocol, two researchers conducted ten to twelve two-hour interviews over a two- or three-day period in each district. Both group and individual interviews were conducted with members of the key groups reflecting all the constituencies of the institution: trustees, CEOs, administrators, faculty, classified staff, and students. The interviews were designed to learn the perceptions of each group about the institution's structures and processes for decision making and communication. We looked at two routine areas—budget making and personnel—and two nonroutine areas—new ideas and unexpected, unpredicted situations. Interviewers transcribed the interview notes into narrative form following the structure of the interview schedule. (See Resource B for examples of the interview materials.)

Preliminary analysis of our data suggested that no single district had a perfect model of the ideal governance system, though each district provided valuable instances of exemplary practices. At this point we became interested in the application of our work to contexts outside of California. We were especially interested in looking at excellent districts in very different political, geographical, and governance contexts. Because of their good reputations, geographical diversity, and size range, we chose three additional districts to add to our data base: Jefferson Community College in Louisville, Kentucky; Miami-Dade Community College in Miami, Florida; and Monroe Community College in Rochester, New York. Jefferson and Miami-Dade had been named in a 1985 study at the University of Texas, Austin, as two of the five best community colleges in the nation for teaching excellence, and Monroe, located in a key state, is a member of the League for Innovation in the Community College and enjoys a fine reputation. The same survey questionnaires and interview schedules were completed at each of these institutions.

This rich data base allowed us to identify several key elements of governance: planning, deciding, acting, reacting, and communicating. Although we treat each element separately, leadership in governance is a complex, paradoxical process that involves planning to decide, deciding to plan, communicating plans, acting on decisions, communicating those actions, reacting to the unplanned, communicating those reactions, and so on. As we demonstrated in this chapter, issues of governance in the community college, the leadership of these institutions, the people that study and work in them, and the environment within which they act, all set in a historical and social context, suggest a kind of Shakespearean "divinity that shapes our ends, rough hew them how we will."

Chapter Highlights

- No decision is context free. Decision-making processes in community colleges occur in particular contexts, two of which are institutional history and social values.

- Community colleges are conceptually and structurally ambiguous institutions.

- In the early decades of this century, junior colleges were created from equal parts of the university moving down and the high school moving up.

- Open-door admissions and acute sensitivity to the needs of students and local communities have created in community colleges quick-response, market-sensitive institutions whose program diversity mirrors the complexity and diversity of society.

- The accumulation of educational functions by community colleges has been the source of much confusion about the nature of the institution both from within and without.

- No simple "animating idea" of the community college has been successfully articulated, a fact which is both a weakness and a strength of the institution.

- The operation of state-level systems as well as of local systems introduces immense new complications into institutional governance and forms the contextual backdrop against which institutions are governed.

- Community colleges have prospered because they have been buoyed by twentieth-century American cultural values, two of which are material prosperity and social equity.

• We believe that institutions move toward the fullest achievement of their potential when they consciously grant their members power, creating the conditions under which more of their members want to do more for the institution.

Part Two

The Role of Leadership in the Decision Process

Chapter Three

Planning

"The best-laid schemes o' mice an' men gang aft agley."
—Robert Burns

Since final decisions are rarely exactly those anticipated in one's plans, and since a truism about plans is that they get changed regularly, it would be easy to see planning as an empty, wasteful exercise. Certainly, unpredictable and irrational events present themselves to community college decision makers with such frequency that spending time on planning can seem a distraction from the important issues facing the institution. Yet, every one of the districts we studied had a clear, well-understood planning process, most often focused on budget and personnel decisions. As we have tried to understand the role of planning in the governance process, we conclude that planning is a critical framework for decision making. While an organizational chart represents the elements of the college in a static way, planning is the dynamic expression of important organizational processes, elements, and relationships. Steven Brandt (1982, p. 98) puts it this way: "The key word is *process*. It implies a continuing, consistent, if not repetitive, sequence of events over time during which the participants can get to know one another, come to share a common vocabulary, and establish a sense of order in the life of the enterprise." Paradoxically, planning is both a framework and a process which itself constitutes a series of decisions. For purposes of our analysis, we treat planning, deciding, acting, reacting, and communicating separately although they are closely interrelated.

We agree with Peters and Austin's (1985) caveat that emphasis on planning techniques (to the exclusion of other

43

dimensions of decision making) is "badly misplaced." They add: "Unfortunately, most innovation management practice appears to be predicated on the implicit assumption that we can beat the sloppiness out of the process if only we can make the plans tidier and the teams better organized" (pp. 114–115).

Principles of Planning

In fact, Peters and Waterman (1982) assert that in trying to understand organizational processes one needs to begin by accepting the limits of rationality. Their views of bounded rationality and an acceptance of the limits of planning as a process for creating the future make sense to us. Peters and Waterman also conceive four basic human needs and principles in organizations that condition the effect of planning in organizational affairs. These principles are that "(1) people need a sense of meaning from their work; (2) people need a modicum of control; (3) people need positive reinforcement, to think of themselves as winners in some sense; and (4) actions and behaviors shape attitudes and beliefs in organizations rather than vice versa" (1982, p. 102). One's expectations of what can be achieved through planning need to be tempered by the complexities of real life. Nevertheless, with all its limitations, planning remains an essential institutional activity.

The nature of planning itself is not mysterious. Each of us plans every day: we have certain *goals* we want to achieve, we identify a number of *needs* related to those goals, we inventory our *resources*. Usually, we find the cost of our needs outstrips our resources, so we are forced to decide on *priorities*. Suppose one wants to create a work space at home. To achieve that goal, one might list such needs as adequate space, quiet, good light, storage capacity, functional equipment, and security. An inventory of resources—existing rooms, furniture, equipment and tools, workbench, shelves, cabinets, time available, money available—would allow matching of needs and resources. One could decide to operate within existing resources, likely leading to postponing or abandoning some of the items on the needs list. Or, one could develop a set of priorities by which time and money would be systematically allocated to creating the desired work space. In a community college, of course, the individual members of the organization have numerous and disparate goals, wide-ranging definitions of need, differing perceptions of resources, and conflicting criteria for establishing priorities. Thus, planning becomes more complex, though the essential elements remain the same.

The Paradox of Planning

Planning is reflective, rational, deliberative. Reality is hectic, stressful, political, emotional, even chaotic. The role of planning is not to eliminate those qualities (that would be impossible) but rather to foster a way of thinking in which various alternatives or scenarios are imagined, allowing decision makers to choose among the possibilities. The number or thickness of planning documents produced is not the measure of good planning. Rather, good decisions with good outcomes are the true measure of one's planning. Planning facilitates effective deciding and acting. A plan, therefore, is not an end. It is a means.

Paradoxically, however, the planning process itself can be an important product if it is carried out sensitively and skillfully. The experience of collaborating in the development of meaningful plans that guide deciding and acting can be enormously energizing. When people genuinely participate in activities that invent the institution's future, they feel empowered, committed to make that future work. Those feelings translate into a better working climate in the organization. On the other hand, if planning is mere busywork and does not guide decision making, the opposite results will be achieved.

Flexibility and adaptability are important qualities of planning. One example of ineffective planning is seen when landscape architects lay out sidewalks according to principles of logic or geometric design, only to find that people make their own paths across the grass or through the landscaping. Planning must account for principles of human conduct and should not be cast in concrete, making it difficult to respond to changing realities. We agree with this dimension of Berg-quist and Armstrong's view of planning: "The key to such a planning process appears to be the recognition that people involved in planning move repeatedly through . . . different conceptual domains . . . and that tendencies toward reflection and action must continually be balanced against one another" (1986, p. 16).

The governance issue at stake in our discussion of planning reflects the paradoxical nature of organizational leadership. Either the paradox will be mismanaged so people feel neglected or powerless or it will be mastered so that people feel they were heard and valued. Thus, on the one hand, a single, finite budget that resolves the many, often conflicting, claims on resources must be prepared each year to ensure the financial health and long-term survival of the college; on the other hand, even when their budget requests have been cut or eliminated, members of the organization should believe that their professional interests, disciplines, and programs are being supported and encouraged. Multicampus districts always face the question of whether decisions will be made at the campus level or at the district level. Even when a central office is assigned the task of coordinating several programs of the same type, the quality of practice still varies and the best program is often found in a single department on one campus. A management structure can assign responsibility for planning, but it cannot predict the source of good ideas or manage the emergence of excellence.

Max DePree proposes a similar paradox in his delightful book, *Leadership Is an Art*. DePree recounts an incident during a church service in which a member of the congregation collapsed. Though none of the many members of the church hierarchy present responded immediately or effectively to the emergency, members of the congregation (including a paramedic, two physicians, and several others) took action to stabilize the victim, call an ambulance, and inform his wife (a choir member). DePree explains the meaning of his anecdote this way:

> The point in telling you this story is to show that while this church has a hierarchy of more than thirty appointed and elected professionals, committee members, board members, and others, the hierarchy did not respond swiftly or decisively. It is difficult for a hierarchy to allow "subordinates" to break custom and be leaders. The people who *did* respond swiftly and effectively are roving leaders. Roving leaders are those indispensable people in our lives who are there when we need them. Roving leaders take charge, in varying degrees, in a lot of companies every day.
>
> More than simple initiative, roving leadership is a key element in the day to day expression of a participative process. Participation is the opportunity and responsibility to have a say in your job and to influence the management of organizational resources based on your own competence and your willingness to accept problem ownership. No one person is the "expert" at everything [1987, pp. 45–46].

Such paradoxes are the norm in complex organizations. At Mt. San Antonio College, Acting President Joseph Zagorski described this cost in their planning process: "Participatory governance is incredibly time consuming. People express frustration—they want things to happen faster." Even in the best of all possible worlds, tension will arise between the impulse simply to get on with it and the desire to plan for actions before they are taken. The planning process must respond to both impulses and must, to some degree, manage the paradox.

In *Leadership in Administration*, Philip Selznick speaks of the "dynamic adaptation of the total organization to internal strivings and external pressures" (1957, p. 31). A sound planning process must account for both "internal strivings" (for example, the competition for resources among organizational units) and "external pressures" (for example, the public's resistance to increased taxes). In fact, the very complexity of the problem suggests that we speak in the plural: planning *processes*. Truly effective planning operates on several levels and in many venues concurrently, all of it guided by the organization's sense of purpose as expressed in its actions.

Monroe Community College demonstrated a sophisticated, sensitive awareness of this complexity in its strategic planning efforts, initiated in 1982 by the recently appointed president Peter Spina and continuing through the time of our study. In its 1986 report the Monroe committee observed, "Effective planning . . . is not dependent upon accurate forecasting. Instead it is precisely when situations are unstable and forecasting most difficult that carefully thought-out plans, flexible enough to adjust to the possible-but-unexpected, are essential" (Osborn, 1986, p. 1). Understanding that having an effect on attitudes and perceptions was an important part of strategic planning, the report notes, "Faculty, staff, and administration would need a broader perspective, one that went beyond each person's particular discipline and training—maybe even beyond each person's past experience. Also we would all need to become accustomed to placing individual planning into a larger framework" (p. 7). The framework that Monroe developed is a model of clarity and adaptability: "Our strategic planning requires that we *re-affirm* those principles we consider basic, *re-think* how they are to be achieved, [and] *re-align* our efforts and emphases to achieve our goals" (p. 9). Among the outcomes Monroe reported were improved quality of decisions, more specific sense of direction, and better positioning to adapt to social and economic changes. Recognizing that recommendations are "rarely the kind to be carried out at the stroke of a pen," the committee described its recommendations "as steering points, focuses for concerted action." The Strategic Planning Committee concluded:

What have we learned? We've learned that a *plan* and *planning* are not the same, any more than they're the same part of speech. The finished *plan* is frozen thought. The value is in *planning*, for it requires stepping outside accepted thinking, seeing in new ways, questioning procedures, regulations, tradition, bureaucratic structures. We've learned the truth of an oriental saying, "The only thing changeless is change." Thus, there never can be a permanent plan; each must be considered temporary, rendered in pencil with large erasers handy. Otherwise the plan itself becomes an obstacle to stifle rather than vitalize.

There is a temptation to accept the façade—explanatory charts, graphs, committees, vocabulary—as the soul. But the soul—the planning—is much harder to specify, for it's found in changed attitudes, expectations, actions, the creation of an environment that enables the organization to spot and solve its problems.

Increasingly our aim is to simplify, to offer "A simple compass—that indicates the general direction and allows us to use our own ingenuity to overcome difficulties" [Osborn, 1986, pp. 25-26].

Characteristics of Planning

As we reflect on our study institutions and our experience, several characteristics of planning emerge. Effective planning is

- Driven by institutional mission and goals
- Action-oriented
- Participative (in both vertical and horizontal dimensions of the enterprise)
- Organizationwide
- Open to accommodate the flow of critical information, ideas, and values
- Structured, but adaptable

Let us illustrate these characteristics by describing how one district approaches planning. In 1979, the Yosemite Community College District established its comprehensive planning process. The process works in annual cycles in the context of five-year plans. The process has been constructed to allow all members of the organization to participate if they choose to do so. To initiate the process, each August the chancellor conducts a workshop meeting with the board of trustees. At this meeting, the district's statement of mission and philosophy is reviewed and fine-tuned. In this context, the board and chancellor approve a set of planning assumptions, including projected growth, cost of living adjustments, and similar factors, which establish ground rules for all units in the organization.

For planning purposes, thirty-five to forty units are identified throughout the organization. Typically, units are defined by function (for example, each academic division is a unit). Every employee is included in a unit, allowing for universal participation in the process, and every unit is responsible to a manager. To maintain flexibility as conditions change in the organization, the process allows for redefinition of a unit. From September through November every year, each unit receives a great deal of data related to its budget, including projections based on previous years' experience. The guidelines encourage each planning unit to think in terms of the ideal, without regard to cost limitations. [Chancellor Tom Van Groningen: "The skeptics said people would go wild, but experience has proven that the process has been taken seriously."] Every unit is required to identify its objectives, its needs for both program resources and personnel, and cost estimates for each. Every unit develops its own approach for identifying its needs and for establishing the priorities among its requests. Each request must be clearly related to the unit's goals and its five-year plan.

Once the unit has produced its budget proposals, they are submitted to the next level, one of three cost centers: Modesto College, Columbia College, and the Yosemite District. Each cost center has established its own process for merging and winnowing the unit plans into a single plan for the cost center. This process usually involves division deans, associate deans, and deans in producing a single plan for their part of the organization; recently, faculty senate leaders have played a role in this integrating process. Again, the specific procedures are not determined centrally, but each cost center must work within the parameters established at the outset by the board and the chancellor. Normally, this process is completed by December.

The three plans are then brought together at the district level, where they are integrated into a single draft budget document during January and February. Typically, the proposed expenditure total runs 5 percent to 10 percent higher than the revenue projections, which have been produced by a different, simultaneous process. [Van Groningen: "Though some might feel it an empty exercise to have each element of the organization state its program needs, knowing that funds are not available to meet them all, we have been able to develop a data base and historical perspective of what it would cost to fully fund our institutional needs. This information has been useful in discussing finance with our community and at the state level."] At this point, the working plan goes back to the three cost centers for further review and discussion of priorities, based on current estimates of revenue. Then, the entire revised document is submitted to the Budget Review Committee, consisting of the college presidents, the chancellor, key business services officials, and both faculty senate and administrative representatives from the colleges. Beginning in 1987, union representatives were invited to sit in during these budget review sessions. By May 1, the tentative budget has been completed and by late May or early June is submitted to the board of trustees where a final review is undertaken.

To establish the importance of the process, budget adjustments (perhaps a result of higher revenue than projected) are made only for items that have been included in a unit's initial plan. Over time, this approach has established credibility, leading more and more members of the district to participate in the process.

The Yosemite comprehensive planning process engages all elements of the organization in identifying current and projected needs, developing organizational consensus around a proposed expenditure budget. Revenue projections are developed in a much smaller and narrower group. The business office supplies data related to various sources of income; the data services office generates projections on future enrollments, both numbers of students and numbers of contact hours. This information is reviewed by a group of ten administrators (the chancellor and his cabinet) before being presented to the board of trustees.

As rational as this process appears, Chancellor Thomas Van Groningen understands the dynamic and ambiguous nature of effective planning: "You never arrive in this business—something is always unfinished and we are willing to live with that uncertainty. We don't demand the 'one big happy family' syndrome. A little tension is healthy in an organization. You need tension on the string in order to make music."

Certainly all the normal tensions exist at Yosemite: two autonomous colleges, one large (Modesto, in the flatlands of the San Joaquin Valley) and one small (Columbia, in the foothills of the Sierra). Part of the district's lore has produced the saying: "Water runs downhill; money runs uphill." Additionally, both the faculty and classified staff are represented by unions in a collective bargaining process. Still, faculty members expressed support for the process: "It helps all of us look at where we want to go: each of us has to sell our agendas to our immediate supervisors. It makes everyone accountable." Classified staff echoed these views: "Comprehensive planning has forced everyone to plan down the road—and we understand that instructional programs are the number one priority."

Effective Planning Processes

As we have looked at planning, several elements of effective processes seem to emerge:

- A broad-based approach to establishing institutional goals
- A credible method for identifying revenue and other resources
- A broad-based approach to developing program needs, costs, and priorities
- An institution-specific set of processes and terms for matching goals, needs, and resources

Effective planning incorporates a way of responding to both *clients* (students and taxpayers) and *constituencies* (departments, programs, employee groups, other interest groups).

Sometimes a planning process is created in response to perceived deficiencies in existing procedures. At Santa Monica College, such a circumstance emerged. Again, impetus for change came from both internal strivings (an overall concern of faculty to be more active in overall college planning) and external pressures (a recommendation from the regional accreditation team encouraging the college to define its long-range planning process more systematically). The model that evolved from repeated discussions among all levels of staff consisted of three collegewide councils (Collegewide Coordinating Council, Dean's Council, and Academic Senate Executive Council) and ten divisional councils (named planning councils) representing functional areas of the college. According to the college president, this planning process was based on one developed by Peter MacDougall, president of Santa Barbara City College.

The first major use of the planning process at Santa Monica focused on the process for deciding which departments would get replacement and new positions for full-time faculty. Prior to 1987, the Department Chairs Committee of the faculty senate heard presentations from each department chair for needs in replacement and new faculty. After the hearings, the committee would prepare a list of recommended positions and send it to senior staff. According to the college president, "there were lies from everyone." Personalities were a dominant factor. All faculty were equal, but English faculty were more equal than vocational faculty. Tension, frustration, and cynicism were the result. Against this backdrop, Santa Monica made use of its new planning councils for developing a priority list of hiring positions.

The process begins at the department level. Both new and replacement positions are treated in the same way—that is, both must be justified in the planning process. Each department proposes to replace a position, to move it to another area of the department, or to create a new position. Written justifications are developed and the proposals go to the division dean, who writes a pro-con analysis for each position. Each of the ten planning councils (representative groups including department chairs, division senators, a counselor, and classified and student members), headed by a division dean in six of the councils or the equivalent for non-academic areas, reviews all the departmental proposals, and produces a ranking. Criteria for the ranking are developed through discussion within each council. Next, the ranked lists with justifications go from the planning councils to the Collegewide Coordinating Council, which, through a process of discussion, develops a single, integrated, ranked list of proposed positions. The senior staff group identifies the budget allocation for positions. In concert with the president, the number of positions is determined and allocated to the departments on the basis of the rank order of the list produced by the Collegewide Coordinating Council. The president reserves the right to revise that list, although he has rarely exercised that right.

The Santa Monica process, similar to the Yosemite process, creates a clear structure that provides a framework for planning; but at each stage of the process, the setting of priorities emerges from the give-and-take of discussion and competing interests. These processes avoid rigid statements, allowing the dynamics of individuals and constituencies to shape the outcomes of planning.

Planning was a dimension of decision making that was easily identified in each study district. Though we are not convinced it is the most important dimension of sound governance and effective leadership, planning carries important symbolic meanings in community colleges. Perhaps Bolman and Deal's conclusion about the role of planning applies: "Planning may not shape the future or inform decisions, but organizations still need to do it. It conveys the impression of foresight and rationality, which encourages outsiders to believe in the organization and to provide support. Planning . . . serves as a stage for important rituals and dramas" (1984, pp. 178–179).

The Yosemite and Santa Monica examples illustrate efforts to incorporate planning into the regular structures and processes of the institution. But often the impulse to plan is a response to the need for change or innovation. When an organization seeks new approaches, the routine processes may be too cumbersome or stifling or may simply be carrying all the load they can bear. In those instances, planning takes place in ad hoc groups (committees, task forces, skunkworks). The Teaching-Learning Project at Miami-Dade Community College fits this description. The genesis of this project is instructive. Most of the key administrators we talked with saw it as the project of President Robert McCabe. And McCabe acknowledged that he put the initial proposal before a faculty group and pledged resources to support it. But faculty leaders we spoke with provided important context: many faculty felt that the existing policies and criteria governing academic rank and promotion were not geared to supporting outstanding teachers. In June 1986 this concern was discussed in the Faculty Senate Consortium, a ten-member group representing the four campuses. McCabe was invited to meet with the group and was asked if he were amenable to some new process being initiated. McCabe's response was that he had a proposal, which he subsequently put before a luncheon meeting of senior faculty (both organizational leaders and chairpersons). As one faculty member described the situation, McCabe said something to this effect: "Here's an idea to address your concern. If you buy in, I'll put new resources into it."

By the fall, the planning process was under way: a search committee of faculty and management selected a director. A steering committee of some twenty people, selected jointly by the president and the consortium president, was established to oversee the effort and to gain commitment throughout the organization. Ultimately, a proposal was developed that was put before the entire faculty in the form of a referendum. The favorable vote produced an innovative program which included a portfolio approach to tenure and promotion decisions and the establishment of endowed teaching chairs. The latter recognized outstanding faculty by providing them with additional funds for carrying out projects of their own devising.

Although many members of the organization viewed this project as a top-down effort being run outside the regular structure and channels of the college decision process, we found that from the outset both "top" and "bottom" found a marriage of interests. Good planning, like good planting, requires both fertile soil and a nurturing environment. To achieve those elements, colleges often develop planning processes unique to a particular issue or problem.

A fine line exists between planning processes that genuinely encourage participation and incorporate the information, ideas, and values generated by participants and those that are used simply to absorb and deflect the energy of critics. For instance, mission and goals statements are sometimes seen in these latter terms. Some blue ribbon committee is commissioned to produce a high-minded statement that neither threatens nor offends anyone. The statement is duly approved, published in the catalogue, used in the accreditation report, and generally ignored. In our view, the development of a mission and goals statement is a critical part of any planning process. Such a statement must be more than words. It must articulate ideas that animate the college. Members of the organization should internalize the spirit of such a statement so that it guides their decisions.

Jefferson Community College provided a good illustration of an approach aimed at gaining such commitment from its staff. Its Institutional Values Project was a campuswide effort to state to the public and the student body what the institution represents. The project engaged faculty and staff broadly in discussions of institutional values. Extending for over a year, this project proposed not only to produce a statement but also to gain wide awareness and acceptance of the philosophy and values expressed by the statement. The results were not only included in the college catalogue but were also distributed to the staff in a series of short memos for that purpose.

A mission statement presents the institution's values in explicit terms. But planning also conveys institutional values, if only implicitly. Since planning takes up time, resources, and people's energy, to make some topic the subject of planning implies that it has been valued over other matters. Thus, a highly participatory budget planning process devoted exclusively to developing expenditure priorities conveys that value to institutional participants. On the other hand, a budget planning process that also includes broad participation in income estimating transmits the value that developing revenue has institutional value on a par with managing expenditures. We think it highly likely that budget decisions will reflect the values inherent in the planning process.

We have argued that planning is a major expression of the rational element in decision making. We see planning as an essential part of the process, one that provides members of the institution a series of frames for considering choices. Planning sets the stage for a more complex aspect of the process, deciding.

Chapter Highlights

• Planning is a critical framework for decision making. While an organizational chart represents the elements of the college in a static way, planning is the dynamic expression of important organizational processes, elements, and relationships.

• Peters and Waterman's view of bounded rationality and their acceptance of the limits of planning as a process for creating the future make sense to us.

• The nature of planning itself is not mysterious. Each of us plans every day: we have certain *goals* we want to achieve, we identify a number of *needs* related to those goals, we inventory our *resources*. Usually, we find the cost of our needs outstrips our resources, so we are forced to decide on *priorities*.

• Planning is reflective, rational, deliberative. Reality is hectic, stressful, political, emotional, even chaotic. The role of planning is not to eliminate those qualities (that would be impossible) but rather to foster a way of thinking in which various alternatives or scenarios are imagined, allowing decision makers to choose among the possibilities.

• Flexibility and adaptability are important qualities of planning.

• Even in the best of all possible worlds, tension will arise between the impulse simply to get on with it and the desire to plan for actions before they are taken. The planning process must respond to both impulses and must, to some degree, manage the paradox.

• Truly effective planning operates on several levels and in many venues concurrently, all of it guided by the organization's sense of purpose as expressed in its actions.

• Effective planning incorporates a way of responding to both *clients* (students and taxpayers) and *constituencies* (departments, programs, employee groups, and other interest groups).

• At each stage of the process, the setting of priorities emerges from the give-and-take of discussion and conflicting interests. These processes avoid rigid statements, allowing the dynamics of individuals and constituencies to shape the outcomes of planning.

• A fine line exists between planning processes that genuinely encourage participation and incorporate the information, ideas, and values generated by participants and those that are used simply to absorb and deflect the energy of critics.

• A mission statement presents the institution's values in explicit terms. But planning also conveys institutional values, if only implicitly. What is made the subject of planning has been valued over other matters since planning takes up time, resources, and people's energy.

Chapter Four

Deciding

"Take care of the small decisions
and the big ones will take care of themselves."
—Traditional saying

Power is exercised in organizations through deciding. This means that everyone exercises power since everyone in every organization makes decisions. In Chapter One, we enumerated several of these ordinary, everyday decisions. Some of them are conscious and deliberate: a faculty member deciding whether to participate on a committee or whether to revise an instructional unit; a president deciding whether to follow up on a suggestion made by a trustee; a union deciding whether to hold out for a 10 percent salary increase regardless of other funding needs in the college. Other decisions may be less deliberate, even unconscious, such as how accommodating a registrar's clerk will be to a confused student, how much effort a groundskeeper will put into grooming a hard-to-reach shrub, how much enthusiasm a dean will have for a project important to the president, in what tone of voice a secretary will address a caller when the phone rings.

These innumerable decisions, in the aggregate, constitute an enormous fund of power, exercised either negatively or positively. This power may operate incoherently, chaotically, without direction, or it may serve institutional purposes. Individual decision making can operate so that it merely serves individual perceptions of need and purpose, thereby creating conflicts or simply confusion. Group decision making can operate purely in the interest of the group, heightening tension and competition for scarce resources. The power inherent in the thousands of decisions made by individuals

60

and groups constitutes a source of energy to be harnessed in the pursuit of the institution's mission. We think this energy constitutes a major institutional resource, one consistently neglected and underutilized. A key task of leadership is to align the isolated, individual power centers of the institution to serve the ends of the enterprise.

When faculty and staff members perceive that officials in the organization are deliberately denying them power or misusing it on them, their "deciding power" will not be fully used to serve the colleges' goals or to contribute the maximum to achieving the institution's mission. Philip Selznick explains this idea:

> The formal, technical system is . . . never more than a part of the living enterprise we deal with in action. The persons and groups who make it up are not content to be treated as manipulable or expendable. As human beings and not mere tools they have their own needs for self-protection and self-fulfillment—needs that may either sustain the formal system or undermine it. These human relations are a great reservoir of energy. They may be directed in constructive ways toward desired ends or they may become recalcitrant sources of frustration. One objective of sound management practice is to direct and control these internal social pressures [1957, p. 8].

Another formulation of this concept can be found in Kieffer and Senge's (1982) discussion of *metanoic organizations*. The term *metanoic* comes from a Greek word which means "a fundamental shift of mind," and Kieffer and Senge use the term to describe a range of contemporary organizational innovations that are based on the unifying principle that "individuals aligned around an appropriate vision can have extraordinary influence in the world" (p. 70). Metanoic organizations, according to these authors, possess a coherent philosophy with five primary dimensions: "1) a deep sense of vision or purposefulness, 2) alignment around that vision, 3) empowering people, 4) structural integrity, and 5) the balance of reason and intuition" (p. 70).

Aligning unique human beings (and the daily decisions they make) around some deeply shared sense of institutional purpose is a daunting assignment. American culture encapsulates the paradox by simultaneously honoring "rugged individualism" and "teamwork," establishing a tension that organizations must manage. Beyond that, the decisions that any individual makes are to a large extent determined by the personality and characteristics of that individual. Some people enjoy a sense of pulling in the same direction with their co-workers; to others alignment feels and sounds like regimentation. Some people are more ambitious and eager to please than others; work is more important to some people than to others; some people are more able and effective than others, and so on.

Yet, the purposes for which community colleges exist and the profound social values upon which their mission rests are important to most of the people who work in community colleges. As a Miami-Dade faculty member said, "I get my satisfaction nurturing students who have not been perceived as college material. I save lives. Just like a doctor. That's my reward. That's why I'm here" (Zwerling, 1988, p. 18). If these purposes and values are articulated in ways and under organizational conditions that people find affirming on a daily basis, they form a kind of magnetic north, drawing the compass needles of organizational participants to it.

Organizational conditions tap into either positive or negative energy in people. Such conditions or climates make people feel good or bad about their work. They tend to evoke commitment or to suppress it. They welcome and reward risk taking or they punish it by making life hard for those whose risks do not succeed. They nurture and reward innovation or they are indifferent or antagonistic to it. So organizational climate affects the extent to which the latent energy or power in the organization can be harnessed to serve the institution's mission.

A number of factors contribute to the creation of such climates. Our research and experience suggest that deciding is a major climate-controlling activity in the community college. The conscious, deliberate acts of deciding by people in official capacities help define a college's climate. At the same time, the unconscious, less deliberate acts of deciding by all members of the organization both reflect and condition that climate. We believe the structures and processes for decision making have a far greater impact on institutional climate than is usually thought. For purposes of this discussion, four interrelated aspects of deciding will be examined:

- The context for deciding
- Preparation for decision making
- The structure for deciding and the content of decisions
- Participation in the processes of deciding

The Context for Deciding

We discussed decision contexts in general terms in Chapter Two. Here we return for a more careful look at the role of context. There are both internal and external contexts for deciding. Externally, for example, the framework of state law and regulation and city or county ordinances exerts powerful influences on institutional decision making. According to Thomas Nussbaum, vice chancellor and general counsel of the California Community Colleges, there are over 2,200 state statutes that directly address community colleges in California, plus an additional 650 regulations of the state's board of governors. New York, in contrast, has a total of 50 statutes, Illinois 275, Oregon 200, Michigan 200, New Jersey 175, Florida 125, Texas 110, Arizona 100, Massachusetts 35, and Ohio 35.

In Oregon, community colleges must submit their budgets to a vote of the electors in the region served by the college. In New York, some community colleges must obtain approval from the county legislatures for the tax millage levies that provide them operating funds. In Pennsylvania, some community colleges are organized as branches of the state university system and others operate independently under a 1963 community college enabling statute. These two types of institutions are organized and compete for resources in two different external contexts. In all states, major policy studies, the work of watchdog agencies and blue ribbon commissions, and media attention are aspects of the external context that can affect internal decision making.

Local communities represent a vital aspect of the external context for deciding. Communities differ in the amount of political and economic support they provide the institution. Relationships between colleges and their communities vary widely. Some years ago the governing board of a community college district located a campus in a municipality that was deeply divided over whether it wished the campus placed there. The mayor of the city opposed the location of the campus in his city. Later, the mayor was elected to the state legislature, and a number of intrusive, highly prescriptive laws affecting all community colleges in the state were introduced by this legislator and subsequently passed.

Internally, the institution's governing board is the single most important entity that shapes the context for decision making. As Kerr and Gade observe: "Boards of lay trustees provide for accountability to the public welfare without government domination (thus institutional autonomy) and for flexibility in operations (thus dynamic adjustments to changing circumstances). Additionally, at least in modern times, such boards provide for mostly nonideological intellectual environments (thus academic freedom), for mixed sources of financing (thus more opportunities for trying new projects and more security in continuing old commitments), and for strong presidencies serving in the name of the board (thus more aggressive leadership)" (1989, p. 10).

In all situations boards are empowered as corporate entities, and individual members have no official authority acting as individuals. In California, a majority vote of the total board, not merely those present, is required for any official action to occur. This means that if only three members of a seven-member board are present at a meeting, no official

action can be taken since four votes are required. Individual
trustees, acting alone, have no official power at all. A single
trustee has no authority to direct that a report be prepared, a
desk be purchased, or a project be undertaken. In the real
world, however, any CEO who is indifferent to the wishes of
individual trustees is not likely to survive long as a CEO.
Fortunately, not all trustees make a practice of personally
intruding upon the CEO or his or her staff. Indeed, the best
trustees do it very rarely. But for those executives whose individual board members require great personal attention and
service, the time required to provide these is given at the
expense of serving institutional processes, among which are
processes for deciding.

Some small boards of five to seven members organize
into subcommittees, a practice that to all but the most sensitive boards is enormously consuming of staff time and which
sometimes invites the kind of intrusion into detailed operations that drains the energies of senior staff members. Other
boards meet every week—a few even more often—again consuming staff resources. One community college board actually
spent time reviewing, in its regular public meeting, the district's telephone bill, call by call. Others review all requests of
any kind for out-of-district travel by any staff member. We
believe that such micromanagement practices on the part of
governing boards do little to ensure accountability; they display a lack of confidence and trust in the staff the board has
employed to serve it, they stultify the growth of any such
trust or confidence, and they virtually ensure a lack of attention to vital issues such as the quality and effectiveness with
which the institution is achieving its mission.

In the most seriously deteriorated situations, one finds
conditions such as those described in a recent report of a
California county grand jury concerning a local school
district:

> The XYZ School District is near insolvency. . . .
> There is no historical evidence to indicate that
> the Board, without outside help, is capable of

making the decisions necessary to turn the District around financially or educationally. . . .

When Board members were interviewed,
each one had a different perception of his/her
responsibilities. Some felt they should be
involved in the daily operation of the District,
others felt they should have contact with school
staff only through the Superintendent. Several
felt their first allegiance was to their local constituency, while others saw their responsibility to
be to the whole District. . . .

Several Board Members hold periodic meetings with site administrators to hear their concerns, totally bypassing the Superintendent.
Board Members continue to have direct contact
with school staff because they feel management
is inflexible and does not respond to their
concerns. . . .

Individual Board Members tend to over-
whelm the Superintendent with innumerable
telephone and written communications. Telephone communication, in particular, has
involved hours-long conversations, which keep
the Superintendent from the responsibility of
managing the District [Grand Jury, 1989].

Fortunately, we are not aware of many situations that
deteriorate into the kinds of calamities just described. Unfortunately, many districts possess one or more of the characteristics mentioned in this grand jury report. Stable, effective
contexts for deciding provide a clear separation of jurisdictions between legislative functions, the purview of the governing board, and executive functions, which should fall to the
CEO and his or her administrative staff.

Traditionally the discussion of differences in roles between board and administration has been framed in terms of
the distinction between policy making and administration. We
believe another useful distinction between the proper roles of

board and administration lies in an analogy to the separation of powers between legislative and executive branches of government. The classic formulation states, "The executive proposes; the legislature disposes." In our state and federal governments, when the system works as designed, the executive makes proposals and recommendations that are disposed of, one way or the other, by the legislature. Following this disposition, the executive implements the action and the role of the legislative body becomes one of oversight, monitoring, and review. Legislative bodies are badly suited, by constitution and temperament, to serve the role of the executive by launching initiatives and setting forth proposals. Since members of the body are all independent and equal, they face the almost irresistible tendency to advance separate proposals. One result of this tendency appears in the proliferation of laws, nowhere more evident, as we noted, than in the state of California. During the implementation, or management, phase of executing policy, when members of the legislating body begin to behave separately as executives, the organization inevitably drifts, its sails flapping. Not only is it impossible for several individuals to steer one vessel, but the collective effect of their efforts also ensures that no one else can steer it. Thus, in institutional governance, where there is a lack of respect for the proper separation of powers, or a lack of clarity concerning the proper functions of each, the context for deciding is confused, unreliable, and inhospitable to sound institutional governance.

The presence or absence of structural elements such as board committees is not a controlling criterion for evaluating a board's effectiveness. Neither is the state of interpersonal relations between individual trustees and staff members, for example, whether board members meet personally or socialize with staff. Committees and personal relationships can be either benign or malignant. The difference seems to emerge from several factors:

- Whether individual trustees have a sense of responsibility to the total institution and do not perceive themselves as representing a particular constituency or program

- Whether their behavior is based on the understanding that they have no authority as individuals or whether they behave as if they were executives in their own right
- Whether they behave with respect for the equal prerogatives of other board members
- Whether their basic motivation for board service is to gratify their own needs (political and ego needs being two common ones) to the neglect of institutional purposes

Governing boards, and individual trustees, create other crucial aspects of the context for deciding. For example, they determine the nature of the subject matter to which executives, and, to a considerable extent, the entire administrative staff, attend. Kerr and Gade state that "the performance of a president depends on the conduct of the board—above almost all else except for the personality and character of the president himself or herself" (1989, pp. 2-3). By the questions they ask, the information they require, and the way they behave interpersonally toward their staff, the board and its members can literally control what the CEO thinks about, how he or she approaches issues, and the recommendations he or she is willing to offer. These factors form an extraordinarily powerful context for deciding in an institution.

Kerr and Gade also acknowledge, however, that "the performance of a board almost equally depends on the conduct of the president" (1989, p. 3). Boards work best in an information-rich environment characterized by full disclosure, in which the board is fully, accurately, and regularly informed concerning all matters that interest it. As one trustee observed when her district's chief executive had failed to keep the board fully informed concerning an important ongoing issue, "The board plays catch-up very badly." When a board feels that it is not being fully informed, or that the information it is receiving is not accurate, it tends to shorten the CEO's leash and may well be drawn across the line from legislative into executive functions. To suggest the power of this principle, we would point to a very different governance situation. In his biography, *Queen Victoria,* Lytton Strachey (1921) contrasts the relations of two prime ministers with the queen. William Gladstone, ever correct and formal, provided his sovereign with the barest sketches of issues facing the government, particularly his cabinet discussions. Victoria, in frustration, frequently meddled in the affairs of government ministers. When Benjamin Disraeli came to power after Gladstone, the new prime minister showered the queen with information, even gossip, from cabinet meetings. With a significantly increased level of information, Victoria allowed Disraeli (and parliament) a much broader scope of action.

Santa Barbara City College gives special attention to the issue of keeping the board well informed. In our interviews with trustees and college president Peter MacDougall, this concern was paramount. The seven-member board has organized itself into three subcommittees: education, finance, and facilities. Each committee has three board members. The assignments change every few years so that board members do not become focused on only one aspect of policy. The subcommittees meet monthly to consider an agenda prepared by the college president. Actions are not taken at these meetings; rather, the emphasis is placed on information and discussion. Staff members and faculty leaders present proposals providing board members the opportunity to ask questions and gather information. According to one board member, "The time in the subcommittee is unrestrained; it provides a mechanism for keeping us informed and allows us the opportunity to buy into and influence policy in the making."

The operation of these and many other factors over time creates significant parts of an institution's history. As we suggested in Chapter Two, there is no more important aspect of the context for deciding than history. History establishes habitual ways of doing things. Habits form and reinforce institutional values, thereby shaping organizational culture. Thus history becomes self-reinforcing: good pasts tend to create good futures, and a bad history is enormously difficult to escape. We think we have found some qualities that contribute to good histories and elaborate them in our final chapter.

The Foothill-De Anza Community College District has enjoyed a good history from its inception in 1957. The communities the district serves are education oriented, largely middle- and upper-middle-class in socioeconomic character, and highly supportive of the college district. Stanford University is located in the district. About three-fourths of the registered voters in the district have taken a class or attended some activity on one or both campuses. The district has not experienced divisive, destructive public controversy over its programs or practices. The board of trustees, reflecting community values, has been committed to high quality from the beginning, in the people it employs, in the facilities it constructs, and in the educational programs it provides. The board, with its stable, long-term membership, has not attempted to achieve this quality cheaply, and has been willing to provide the financial resources that such quality requires.

In the years immediately following the passage in 1978 of California's tax revolt initiative, Proposition 13, the good history of the district was interrupted. A bitter dispute arose between the faculty union and the administration, and relations deteriorated to an unprecedented low. In 1985 Cyril Gulassa, who became the union president after the hostilities had ended, wrote about this earlier period:

> The District Board and faculty were in bitter, protracted conflict. We went through impasse, factfinding; the board unilaterally imposed its contract on us; we filed with the Public Employee Relations Board. We were in the process of implementing sanctions and cranking up the only real weapon faculty have—the strike.
>
> In one of the darker hours, we agreed with our chancellor that when the crisis was over, we had to invent a better way to deal with each other than that provided by the industrial model of collective bargaining. At the last moment we both pulled back and resumed negotiations. We were genuinely awed by our power to destroy

not so much each other, but our collective
achievement and the sense of professional well-
being and common mission that makes work
rewarding in itself. We discovered that we were
part of a greater whole than the sum of ourselves
[1985, pp. 39–40].

The compelling sense of this "collective achievement,"
created by Foothill-De Anza's good history, guided the district's leadership—faculty, board, administration—toward
restoring amity and creating a good future. It was analogous
to Selznick's notion of the "distinctive competence" that an
organization acquires over time (1957, p. 42). When history
provides no such guidance, or when its counsel is negative
and a "distinctive inadequacy" has been acquired, creating a
good future that is a congenial context for deciding, we
believe, is a great deal more difficult.

Preparing to Decide

Before most significant decisions are taken there is a period of
preparation during which dominant roles are played by three
factors: information, personalities, and political pressures. The
modern information industry, wishing to cast information as
the lead player, cooperates with decision makers who wish
their decisions to appear highly rational and data based. Thus
managers and the information industry develop a relationship
that arguably constitutes a community college analogue to the
"military-industrial complex" about which President Dwight
Eisenhower warned the nation. In this relationship almost
magical powers are ascribed to information systems. Birnbaum
explains this phenomenon at People's Community College:
"At People's . . . the development of management information
systems created large quantities of data that then required further interpretation and explanation. This led to a need for
more data and the hiring of people who believed in the importance of collecting and analyzing information. As a result,
People's allocated significant resources to its management infor-

mation system, although the system itself is now so complex that managers find it virtually useless for their daily needs. The importance of such information is one of the rational myths of the college" (1988, p. 117).

Information, of course, is crucial to decision making. During the period of preparing to decide, information plays a vital role. Accurate, complete information allows decision makers to see the complexities in a decision, to consider trade-offs and risks, and to establish a shared basis for deciding and acting. This is true whether the decision involves an individual who is deciding which video recorder to buy, or whether it is an institutional decision concerning a new mainframe computer system. But it is also true that personalities and competing interests within the institution shape and use information as a tool to achieve their own objectives. There are those who argue both for and against each of these institutional decisions. Both groups of advocates constitute competing interests. Accommodating such interests depends less on information than on personalities and political pressures.

In Chapter One, we discussed the role of personalities in governance. In the specific act of deciding, personalities vary greatly both in the use they make of information and in their reaction to the pressures brought by individuals and groups. Personalities play a key role in determining the amount and kind of pressure brought to bear on decisions. Most decisions in organizations do not involve choices between good things and bad things; most are choices among competing "goods." In many of the most difficult decisions— for example, whether to grant tenure to a faculty member about whom there is some question—the information available is often ambiguous and contradictory. In other cases when choices must be made, such as whether to buy an auto-clave for the biology department or a metal lathe for the machine tool technology program, information may support the purchase of both, thus compounding the problem of deciding. Personalities and politics loom large in many such decisions, however rational decision makers may attempt to appear.

Personalities are involved in decisions in other ways. Some individuals make even the most difficult decisions quickly; others seem unwilling ever to come to closure on an issue. Some persons decide in private, seeking advice from few, if any, counselors; others consult widely and in some cases engage in what amounts to public decision making. Some individuals give the impression they are making decisions in consultation arenas only later to change their decisions unilaterally after talking to someone else. For some, decisions seem to be a function of whom they talked to last. Individuals vary widely in the level of detail they consider in decision making: some people focus principally on forests, others on trees. Some individuals are extraordinarily effective in "positive" decision making, such as creating new programs or building facilities, but do not do well in "negative" decision making, such as cutting back, reducing force, or retrenching. Other personalities are just the opposite. Some personalities are scrupulously fair and impartial in making decisions; others use decisions as weapons and rewards, punishing their enemies and dispensing largesse to their friends. At the base of it, institutions are as subjective as individuals when deciding. This means that all concepts of unbounded rationality and the controlling role of information are misleading.

Granting the powerful role of both personality and politics, colleges still must prepare to decide. The Santa Barbara City College process we mentioned above illustrates several important elements of preparing. First, the board meets with the college president three times a year in retreats. These retreats "allow us to define our objectives; we don't have to make decisions," reported one trustee. One kind of objective that is articulated at these sessions is parameters for budget development, such as these priorities: (1) safety, (2) 5 percent reserve, and (3) no staff layoffs. The president then conveys these principles in his message to budget developers. Later, after faculty and staff have developed their budget proposals through a multilevel process of the type we described for Yosemite district, the board will review budget drafts in subcommittee. This provides the occasion for board members to understand the needs of the college as well as to monitor the way board priorities have been built into the budget. It also provides opportunities for both the board and the staff to become informed and to work on resolution of conflicts of values, personalities, and competing interests. One trustee summed up: "In the retreats, we talk to each other; in the subcommittees, we talk to the college and with the college." All of this talk precedes the occasion, at a public board meeting, in which a policy proposal comes under consideration for discussion and formal decision.

The Structure for Deciding and the Content of Decisions

Structures for decision making emerge in colleges both as a consequence of rational choices that certain functions need to be performed (thus, for example, curriculum committees are created) and as a result of the operation of natural forces within institutions, often involving the competing interests of the parties (thus, for example, the particular membership of a given curriculum committee is determined).

In some ways the vocabulary of community college decision making is remarkably similar across institutions. All have lay governing boards, usually called boards of trustees. Most have a group called the president's cabinet or council; most have faculty or academic senates; many have unions that represent faculty and support staff; most have academic councils or petition committees that administer grading, academic probation, and academic disqualification regulations; most have curriculum committees, and so on.

In other ways the vocabulary of decision-making groups is unique to each institution. Monroe Community College has its Academic Governance Board (AGB), Santa Monica has the Three Presidents (current president, immediate past president, and president-elect of the academic senate), Jefferson Community College has the "8 Group" (the president, business manager, and six senior administrators), Foothill-De Anza has the Budget and Policy Development

Group (BPDG), Miami-Dade has the Faculty Senate Consortium (the campus senate presidents plus additional faculty members depending on the size of each campus faculty), Santa Barbara has its College Planning Council (CPC), Allan Hancock has its Academic Planning and Programming (AP&P) Committee, Mt. San Antonio has its College Council, and the Yosemite Community College District has its District Council.

Unique structures such as these emerge from three factors: the distinctive history and culture of each institution, the adaptations made by the particular organization to the special needs and issues that confront the organization, and the personalities and personal preferences of the people in the institution, most central of whom is the chief executive officer. These three factors also control the content of the decisions that are made within the various structures.

At Allan Hancock College, the revenue estimates for a given budget year are arrived at by President Gary Edelbrock and the vice president of administrative services. The assumptions for revenue estimating come from the vice president's knowledge of revenue history and the president's knowledge of board priorities and likely levels of support from the state. These assumptions are not generally part of the budget discussions engaged in by members of the institution. At Foothill-De Anza Community College District, both the assumptions behind revenue estimates and the actual revenue projections are regularly reviewed and discussed in the Budget Policy and Development Group, a broadly representative entity that serves as the chancellor's cabinet. This participatory structure ensures that revenue estimates will be subjected to review and examination by people representing all major constituencies of the colleges.

The variation we found in our community college study districts mirrors the variety across American community colleges. In most institutions a great many of the decisions to be made involve comparable subject matter, but the venues within which such decisions are made and the participants in the process differ considerably.

Participation in the Processes of Deciding

In the same way that the structures for deciding and the content of decisions in the various structures differ from place to place, the players also vary. Some of the most interesting variations among institutions arise in the nature and the extent of participation in deciding. In *How Colleges Work* Birnbaum (1988) sketches descriptive portraits of four types of postsecondary institutions. These portraits provide a useful comparative context for our discussion of participation in decision making in the community college.

Heritage College, a 150-year-old, 1,150-student liberal arts college, is described as a "collegial" institution in which "an emphasis on consensus, shared power, common commitments and aspirations, and leadership that emphasizes consultation and collective responsibilities are clearly important factors" (Birnbaum, 1988, p. 86). Hierarchical structures are minimized at Heritage. The president is seen not as boss but as first among equals. The faculty and members of the administration at Heritage "consider each other as equals, all of whom have the right and opportunity for discussion and influence as issues come up. . . . *Decisions are ultimately to be made by consensus, and not by fiat, so everyone must have an opportunity to speak and to consider carefully the views of colleagues*" (1988, p. 88; emphasis added).

Regional State University (RSU) has evolved from a state normal school to a state teachers' college, to a state college, and finally into one of five comprehensive public universities controlled by a statewide board of regents. In contrast to Heritage, RSU is described as a "political" system, "a supercoalition of subcoalitions with diverse interests, preferences, and goals" (Birnbaum, 1988, p. 132). In decision making at RSU, "administrators have power through their access to budget and personnel procedures, to sources of information and to internal and external legal authority; faculty and other professionals have power related to their specialized expertise, to tradition, and to external guilds. Clerical and blue-collar groups may invoke the power of their unions in order to influence policies. And, as the example of a campus women's caucus demonstrates, it is possible for groups to obtain power through informal contacts and through appeals based on moral or ethical principles, such as equity" (p. 134). *At RSU decision making has become diffused and decentralized and "the power to get one's way comes neither from norms nor from rules but is negotiated"* (p. 130; emphasis added).

Flagship University enrolls 27,500 students in its two undergraduate colleges, graduate school, and six professional schools. The university also operates a number of research centers and institutes. Birnbaum (1988) characterizes Flagship as an "organized anarchy." Governance processes seem "dictated largely by intuition, irrational precedent, and from-the-hip responses." Decisions, concerning resource allocation, for example, are made "by whatever process emerges . . . but without reference to some superordinate goals. The 'decisions' of the system are a consequence produced by the system but intended by no one and decisively controlled by no one" (p. 153). The faculty and officers of the administration are key participants in decision making. They are free to participate in many decisions if they are willing to expend the time and energy. They are also free not to participate. As a consequence, *participation in decision making is "fluid," such that "there are probably few, if any, occasions on which decisions on two related issues are made by the same people"* (p. 156; emphasis added).

People's Community College enrolls about 6,000 degree students and is located in a middle- and working-class suburb of a large metropolitan area. People's is described as a "bureaucratic" institution in which there is conscious and rational effort "to link means to ends, resources to objectives, and intentions to activities" (Birnbaum, 1988, p.113). Bureaucracies, of course, are hierarchical, which means that people close to each other on the organization chart tend to interact more frequently; thus "administrators spend little time with faculty and talk instead to other administrators and to external nonfaculty audiences" (p. 107). At the top of the hierarchy is the president who is "expected to be a rational analyst who can not only calculate the most efficient means by which goals can be achieved but also design the systems of control and coordination that direct the activities of others" (p. 124). The president plays a dominant role in decision making at People's. Birnbaum describes People's faculty as "less professional" than faculty in the other institutions since only 10 percent have doctorates. He says, "They are also more likely to have had experience in secondary school systems and therefore to have been socialized to expect less involvement in decision making. *As long as [the president] is seen as equitably administering institutional processes, as consulting with faculty even though reserving to himself the right to make final decisions, as maintaining or expanding institutional resources, and as providing for the faculty's own economic interests through fair dealings with their union representatives, his leadership at People's is likely to be accepted"* (p. 127; emphasis added).

No institution, of course, is a pure example of its dominant form. For example, there are collegial aspects of Regional State, anarchical aspects of Heritage, political aspects of People's, and bureaucratic aspects of Flagship. But these useful portraits suggest enormously important cultural differences across institutional types in American higher education. Our research and experience suggest there are equally important differences among institutions of the same type. In almost every community college elements of bureaucratic, collegial, political, and anarchical functioning may be found. The mix and the interrelationships among them define the special cast of characters and unique ways in which each institution decides.

Estela Bensimon (1989) suggests an emerging trend among newer CEOs in community colleges toward fostering greater participation in decision making. Using Birnbaum's institutional typology to assess "good presidential leadership," Bensimon studied the "espoused theories" of leadership of thirty-two college and university presidents, including five from community colleges. She classified the presidents' stated interpretations of good presidential leadership into bureaucratic, collegial, political, or symbolic frames of reference.

Thirteen of the presidents expressed points of view dominated by only one of the four frames; eleven were classified as having "paired-frame" orientation; eight responded in ways that Bensimon classified as "multiframe." Though her sample of thirty-two—only five from community colleges—is quite limited, her analysis is suggestive. One striking finding "is that universities, public comprehensive colleges, and independent colleges appear in all three [types of frames] . . . ; community colleges, on the other hand, converge in single-frame theories" (Bensimon, 1989, p. 117). She suggests that theories espoused by community college presidents concentrate in the single-frame category because the colleges are aligned with the bureaucratic model of governance. But she finds that the results of the study do not support this commonly accepted view:

> Only two of the five community college presidents with a single frame had a bureaucratic orientation. The other three had either collegial or symbolic frames.
>
> The finding that four out of the five single-frame theories espoused by community college presidents have either a bureaucratic or collegial orientation may reveal tendencies to view the organization as a closed system. Presidents of community colleges are perhaps prone to closed system views because decision-making is centralized; and they, rather than the faculty, control transactions with the external environment.
>
> Furthermore, three of the five community college presidents with a single-frame orientation were recent appointees; and none of them had a bureaucratic orientation. The two who did had served in their positions for some time. Possibly, as George Vaughan had suggested, the newer generation of community college presidents favors leadership approaches encouraging greater participation and shared decision-making [Bensimon, 1989, pp. 119–120].

Our research did not pose questions to the presidents of the institutions in our study that compare to Bensimon's questions. Furthermore, the presidents we questioned were not "newer generation" CEOs. Compared to their counterparts in other institutions, they were quite senior. So we do not know how these individuals might view leadership in terms of the four organizational frames of reference. We can say, however, that a dominant orientation to leadership of almost all our study presidents was toward encouraging greater participation and shared decision making.

Chapter Highlights

- Power is exercised in organizations through deciding. This means that everyone exercises power since everyone in every organization makes decisions.

- These innumerable decisions, in the aggregate, constitute an enormous fund of power, exercised either negatively or positively. This power may operate incoherently, chaotically, without purpose, or it may serve institutional purposes.

- Leadership requires aligning the isolated, individual power centers of the institution to serve the ends of the enterprise.

- Organizational climate affects the extent to which the latent energy or power in the organization can be harnessed to serve the institution's mission.

- Deciding is a major climate-controlling activity in the community college.

- Local communities make up a vital aspect of the external context for deciding.

- Internally, the institution's governing board is the single most important entity that shapes the context for decision making.

- Stable, effective contexts for deciding provide a clear separation of jurisdictions between legislative functions, the proper purview of the governing board, and executive functions, which should fall to the CEO and his or her administrative staff.

- Boards work best in an information-rich environment characterized by full disclosure, in which the board is fully, accurately, and regularly informed concerning all matters that interest it.

- Establishing good habits and good history is analogous to Selznick's notion of the "distinctive competence" that an organization acquires over time. When history provides no such guidance, or when its counsel is negative and a "distinctive inadequacy" has been acquired, creating a good future that is a congenial context for deciding is a great deal more difficult.

- Before most significant decisions are made there is a period of preparation during which dominant roles are played by three factors: information, personalities, and political pressures.

- Structures for decision making emerge in colleges both as a consequence of rational choices that certain functions need to be performed and as a result of the operation of natural forces within institutions, often involving the competing interests of the parties.

- Some of the most interesting variations among institutions arise in the nature and the extent of participation in deciding.

- In almost every community college vestiges of bureaucratic, collegial, political, and anarchical functioning may be found. The mix and the interrelationships among them define the special cast of characters and the unique ways in which each institution decides.

- We can say, however, that a dominant orientation to leadership of almost all of our study presidents was toward encouraging greater participation and shared decision making.

Chapter Five

Acting

"And thus the native hue of resolution
Is sicklied o'er with the pale cast of thought,
And enterprises of great pitch and moment
With this regard their currents turn awry
And lose the name of action."
—Hamlet

Planning is a framework for deciding. Deciding is a mechanism for setting direction, for gaining alignment among an institution's people. But all of that is for nothing if it "lose the name of action." The whole point of effective decision making is to produce good outcomes. The most obvious outcomes are that students learn and grow, complete courses, and earn degrees. But other outcomes are important: that faculty feel challenged and valued in their work; that administrators and support staff believe what they do makes a difference; that board members and the community at large believe that they are receiving a good return on their investment of money, time, and effort.

Peters and Waterman (1982) list a "bias for action" as one characteristic of high-performing companies. Bolman and Deal summarize that characteristic:

> A "bias for action" means that the effective companies did not get bogged down in endless paperwork and bureaucratic entanglements. When they were not sure something would work, they conducted a quick, small experiment rather than a two-year research project. The motto seemed to be, "Act first and learn from the results," rather

than trying to anticipate and solve every problem
before doing anything. An action tendency is a
potential antidote to two constant dangers: the
constraining and dulling effects of the "dead
hand of structure" and the pervasiveness of uncertainty and ambiguity. An organization that
requires everyone to fully justify every course of
action before doing anything is likely to be an
organization that never does anything new or different. . . . "Bias for action" becomes a symbol of
a culture that supports creativity and risk taking
[1984, pp. 280–281].

The Teaching-Learning Transaction

Since the heart of a community college (indeed, any educational institution) lies in what happens in the minds, perhaps
even the souls, of its students and faculty, the institution has
a natural bias toward thought and reflection. Colleges do not
really have the equivalent of profit margins, sales quotas, or
the sales meeting, all of which intend to galvanize salespeople
to action. But within the context of higher education, community colleges have generally seen themselves as *action-oriented*. "[Flathead Valley College] understands that among the
associations, churches, unions, businesses, service clubs and
public agencies of its small town, it alone is able to provide
many of the services that people need, and it has accepted
that role with uncharacteristic vigor. Perhaps this sense of
itself is best summed up by the veterinarian who is chairman
of the trustees: 'Whatever people want,' he says, 'we'll give
'em' " (Van Dyne, 1973, p. 55). This notion of action usually
refers to the college's responsiveness to its local community,
job market, and identified student needs. Community colleges
have the reputation of developing and implementing programs very quickly, a characteristic seen as admirable by
many, but often a source of criticism. "In [the two-year colleges'] haste and fervor for putting courses into prisons and
storefronts, for adult education and remedial education, they

have lost sight of the academic focus. With some exceptions they're trying to do everything for everybody, and there's a growing concern at the state level that they've created a kind of monster that just keeps growing" (Breneman and Nelson, 1980, p. 81). L. Steven Zwerling offers a more balanced perspective on the relation of reflecting and acting in one of our study institutions: "Administrators also emphasized how the Miami-Dade process of reform is a patient one—it is not unusual to study major issues for three years, then take five more to implement them. When I said that my experience taught me that waiting too long killed the inspiration, they insisted that taking time was necessary to build consensus. McCabe had made a 'commitment' to survey everyone regularly about every significant initiative and to respond directly to every idea, every criticism" (1988, pp. 19–20).

The central action of any community college, the teaching-learning transaction of the classroom and laboratory, is not easily viewed or assessed. Traditions of academic freedom protect teachers from intrusion by the public or media. The art of teaching is sufficiently complex and diverse that simple observations in a classroom may not give evidence to the action, certainly not in the same way that observing disk drives coming off an assembly line or checks arriving in the mail are evidence of action in a company. The act of learning, though it has many behavioral manifestations, remains out of view, occurring in the mind of the learner, and our instruments for assessing that learning are highly inexact. Evan Watkins, in an analysis of "work time" in English departments, illustrates the scope and complexity of determining what students do, much less knowing what they have learned from what they do:

> Let's assume a university English department with 50 faculty (temporary, tenure-track, tenured), 3 full-time clerical workers, 3 administrators, and 5 work-study students. For simplicity, assume further that faculty, administrators, and clerical workers all work an average 40-hour week in

whatever variety of tasks during the 30 weeks of
the school year, and the work-study students an
average of 12 hours a week. That yields a total of
69,000 hours of labor time during the school year,
exclusive of summer. Keeping things here to a
minimum, on the average assume each faculty
member has 50 students in classes during the
course of the entire school year, and that those 50
students average 4 hours a week, including class
time of course, on all their assigned tasks in English. That yields 300,000 hours of total labor time
during the school year, more than four times as
much as faculty, administrators, work-study students, and clerical combined. By far the greatest
percentage of total labor time in English is generated by a work force [which spends only a frac-
tion of its time in the workplace itself] [1989,
pp. 23–24].

As Watkins suggests, ordinarily, the total work of students is
not directly accounted for. Rather, the actions most often
focused on by community college decision makers tend
toward matters that relate to financial accountability: student
enrollments, student achievements (number of graduates,
transfers, program completers), course offerings, teacher scheduling and related work load measures, and compensation.
The danger exists, of course, that these observable, countable
actions assume a value greater than their true worth to the
teaching-learning exchange. In fact, the real issue may be
just which actions in a community college do count and the
problem for decision makers becomes determining which
actions to count.

Doing Things Right/Doing the Right Things

A current cliché in discussing organizations claims that the
distinction between management and leadership lies in the
aphorism, "Management tries to do things right. Leadership

tries to do the right things." Of course, in any successful organization, the goal is to do the right things right. But how does one assess "right"? And who participates in determining what is "right"? These questions seem more easily answered in the tangible aspects of organizational life. For instance, "doing the right thing" in relation to faculty salaries may mean ensuring that those salaries are competitive with salaries in colleges of comparable size and circumstance. The actions related to such a goal probably involve information gathering, discussion of the data by the board of trustees, negotiating teams or salary committees, agreement on a percentage increase that will produce the desired result, and, finally, formal agreement by the board of trustees to that percentage. "Doing things right" in this situation involves prompt and accurate changes in the paychecks received by the faculty. Actions related to this purpose include modifying the payroll program that generates checks, testing the modifications for errors, perhaps even authorizing overtime pay for payroll staff to ensure timely, accurate paychecks. In such a situation, the actions that flow from decisions seem clear, easy to predict, and relatively easy to assess.

But how can this be applied to the educational program? Suppose that in a particular college "doing the right things" means increasing the number of ethnic minority students who transfer to four-year colleges. What actions should flow from this intention? Without a blueprint or a documented history of successful practice, how does one do things right? Should the college president call a meeting of the staff and give a speech intended to persuade faculty and support personnel to accept this goal? Should a new program focusing on minority student transfers be created? Should information on the relative rates of transfer of different demographically defined groups be provided to all faculty? Should exemplary programs be visited? Should research be conducted to determine whether some faculty are already succeeding in this area? Should all these actions be taken? If so, how should one decide which actions to take first and which to take later? What about initiating all the actions simultaneously and simply seeing which seems most promising? In such a context, what does "doing things right" mean?

Loosely and Tightly Coupled Systems

One of the useful conceptual tools for addressing these questions comes from Karl Weick's view of "educational organizations as loosely coupled systems" (1976, p. 1). By loose coupling, Weick (p. 12) means that "coupled events are responsive, but that each event also preserves its own identity and some evidence of its physical or logical separateness," adding that "their attachment may be circumscribed, infrequent, weak in its mutual effects, unimportant, and/or slow to respond." Weick contrasts "loosely coupled systems" with "tightly coupled systems" and speculates that "it may be the *pattern* of couplings that produces the observed outcomes." In terms of the example above, salary negotiations, formal agreement, and the payroll system are all tightly coupled (parties negotiate, board approves, president directs, payroll department complies). On the other hand, the actions required to increase minority student transfer rates are loosely coupled (leaders articulate goals, task groups try to develop information and concepts, departments propose programs and courses, some faculty members change some behaviors in relation to students). In the tightly coupled example, the series of actions that flow from the decision must occur in a prescribed sequence but in the loosely coupled case any one of the actions could occur before or after any other of the actions.

These concepts—tight coupling and loose coupling—can guide decision makers who want to do the right things and do things right. For example, in matters where timing is essential (getting students registered, getting paychecks to employees), actions that are tightly coupled will likely lead to doing a good job. On the other hand, in matters where thoughtful judgment, creativity, and academic values are paramount (writing curriculum, selecting textbooks), actions that are loosely coupled will produce more desirable results.

The table of organization usually conveys a picture of tight coupling, but the actual behavior of participants is usually more loosely coupled. Each decider, consciously or unconsciously, establishes criteria of when simply to act or when to follow the formal structure, seeking approval through "the chain of command." Deciders with a clear sense of institutional purpose, determining that a proposed act is consistent with that purpose, are able to act expeditiously. On the other hand, deciders who focus on procedures rather than purposes may be reluctant to act without some confirmation by a higher authority.

We have distinguished *acting* from *deciding* and *reacting*. A brief clarification of the distinction may help readers understand the focus of these separate discussions. *Acting* takes place during the ordinary processes and predictable events in the conduct of affairs in community colleges; *reacting* occurs when nonroutine, unpredictable situations arise and require decision making. As we discussed in Chapter Four, *deciding* has two dimensions: (1) the myriad of individual choices that each member of the organization makes on a daily basis; (2) the institutional governance processes which, if properly led and managed, can be used to align those choices around a college's values, its mission and goals. Thus, in real situations, *deciding* has a complex relationship with both *acting* and *reacting*. Much of the business of leadership lies in understanding those complexities in a given community college. For instance, producing a schedule of classes is a predictable, routine process in which the flow of planning, deciding, and acting is well understood by decision makers. But if an asbestos problem made a large classroom building unusable, this event would disrupt usual procedures. Decision makers would need to react to the crisis. One likely goal would be to take actions that would, as quickly as feasible, restore the scheduling process to normal routine. One of the marks of effective leadership lies in knowing what situations require reacting, thereby setting in motion nonroutine decision and communication processes, and which situations require acting, merely directing individuals and groups into the usual decision process. Misjudgments can lead to under-reacting or overreacting, which may generate even greater problems than the event that led to reacting.

To illustrate, a faculty member had established a pattern of meeting with classes only briefly and then dismissing them. In a critical instance, the faculty member had an evening class at an off-campus site that was scheduled to meet for four hours once a week. On several occasions, she met with the class briefly, assigned them tasks in groups, and then left—students were on their own and had no way of checking back with the instructor. When student complaints brought this situation to the attention of the dean, he could simply have acted according to existing procedures, first counseling the faculty member, then documenting the instructor's failure to meet classes if the pattern continued, docking her pay, and giving a written reprimand. Instead, the dean overreacted by calling the instructor to his office, berating her for a whole series of alleged past failings in the conduct of other classes, and challenging her competence as a teacher. The faculty member went to the professional relations committee, complaining that the dean was harassing her. Because the dean had not acted according to regular procedures, he was vulnerable to such criticism. Although the problem with the faculty member appeared clear-cut, the dean's reaction complicated and confused the situation. Ultimately, no disciplinary action was taken against the faculty member.

Put simply, acting is doing. By its nature, action is of the moment, ephemeral. Its importance in the process of decision making lies in its relationship to other elements: How does what is done relate to what was *planned?* How does what is done connect to what was *decided?* In reality, acts flow from plans and decisions and, in turn, shape plans and decisions. Thus, one looks both forward and backward from the point of action.

Evaluation as a Form of Acting

Every decision-making process must establish some means for knowing what relations exist among planning, deciding, and acting. The conventional term for these means is *evaluation*. Evaluation is a distinctive form of acting, one that requires stepping out of the usual flow of events to make judgments and assess outcomes. In this context, evaluation serves three purposes: determining that action occurred (someone did something), determining that the action that occurred was the one intended, determining that the action produced the intended result.

In human organizations, intentions and actions rarely match up perfectly. If planning and deciding are the arenas in which intentions are expressed, then *implementation* (a common term for acting) is the place where intentions find the name of action, and evaluation is the arena where actions are assessed. Our observation suggests that even colleges with reasonably effective governance arrangements are more conscious of the processes of planning and deciding than the processes of implementing and evaluating. Typically, actions are evaluated in relation to intentions. Success is thought to be achieved when implementation conforms with intentions expressed in the planning process. For instance, if the decision arrived at was to create a minority student transfer program, each academic area might be called on to report increases in minority enrollments in transfer courses. These reports would be consolidated into a collegewide report that would demonstrate what percentage of success had been achieved in relation to the goals stated in the original plan for the program (assuming that explicit, measurable goals had been articulated at the outset). The evaluation actions in this example emphasize data gathering and reporting in categories determined prior to actual implementation. Thus, the effectiveness of the evaluation depends on how well the variables chosen to measure success reflect what actually happens to students (for example, they actually transfer).

Another commonplace form of evaluation, more recently called "management by wandering around" (MBWA) by Peters and Waterman (1982), proceeds from a different set of assumptions. In this case, the test of one's plans and decisions is found in the personal observation of actions occurring in the organization. Here, what teachers and students are actually doing becomes the starting point of assessment. Decision makers spend time observing and participating "where the action is." This approach, though messier and more anecdotal, allows decision makers to see directly whether what was intended in the planning and deciding phases of a program manifests itself in the behaviors and expressed attitudes of faculty and students. This approach also permits decision makers to see how the law of unintended consequences applies to the decision made: Are the results what the planners imagined? Where results are not those anticipated in the plan, are those results better, worse, or simply different from those intended?

Every community college has both tightly coupled and loosely coupled elements, and many community colleges employ both formal and informal approaches to evaluation. The challenge for leadership, the goal of the governance process, is to find the appropriate mix of tight coupling and loose coupling, the balance between data-based evaluation reports and the direct assessment provided by personal observation. For instance, the procedures for handling cash in college operations best fit the tightly coupled compliance model of accountability. Even one case of mishandling cash receipts is unacceptable. Encouraging every unit that takes in cash to experiment with procedures invites trouble. Thus, measuring each cash operation against a single set of predecided control procedures is an appropriate form of evaluation. On the other hand, a math department head who issued a set of accountant-type prescriptions that were intended to reduce the dropout rate in calculus classes would likely find that approach ineffective. Some faculty would resist simply on the principle of academic freedom; some would comply in a mechanistic way that would adhere to the letter of the prescriptions but not to the intended purpose; some would simply reinterpret the prescriptions as suggestions and employ those that seemed to fit their students' characteristics and their own teaching style; some would have evidence that they already were doing a better job in this regard than most of their colleagues and would feel justified in ignoring the prescriptions.

Robert Birnbaum, in *How Colleges Work,* describes this kind of evaluation in terms of explicit and implicit control systems in his fictional ideal of an effectively run institution, Huxley College:

> Activities at Huxley College are regulated by two kinds of control systems that operate within constraints established by the organizational culture. These control systems function as "organizational thermostats." The first system consists of explicit controls manifested in organizational rules, regulations, and structures. These are structural controls. For example, when a department at Huxley attempts to make expenditures beyond its budget (and therefore to move outside the area of acceptability), the purchase order is immediately returned marked "account overdrawn," and the budget is returned to its balanced and desired state.
>
> The second kind of system includes implicit controls developed through the interaction of individuals in groups that lead them toward shared attitudes and concern for group cohesion. These are social controls. They can be seen, for example, as Department Chair Chippendale says to Professor Branch, "Students seem to be upset that some people in the department haven't been available for advisement lately" (noting the receipt of input that an important value has moved outside the range of acceptability), and Branch responds with a look of concern that confirms the importance of advisement and that strengthens their agreement about it [1988, p. 182].

Birnbaum notes that "structural controls and social controls are organizational feedback loops that are sensitive to selected factors in the environment" (pp. 182–183). Thus, both the compliance approach and the informal monitoring approach can be seen as sensing systems that respond to critical factors, as defined by college officials. In brief, *intent* (often expressed in plans) may lead to *control systems* (often expressed in policies or rules) that may be either tightly or loosely coupled mechanisms providing a context for actions producing results that may be evaluated (and may loop back to control systems).

In one community college a number of years ago, the lowest level of remedial English was prescriptively organized. A coordinator produced daily lesson plans, complete with assigned readings and exercises, to be used by everyone teaching the course. Individual instructors were provided these plans on a weekly basis with the clear expectation that they would be carried out according to the schedule. Though such an approach seems to ensure common standards in a department, the learning process is not so neat. On one occasion, the daily lesson was devoted to an exercise in distinguishing fact from opinion. The exercise, as stated in the departmental lesson plan, was designed so that students would treat matters of opinion as fact. The suggested methods all proceeded from this assumption. But in one class, the opposite occurred. Students readily identified opinion as opinion, but frequently identified facts as opinions. About halfway through the exercise, the instructor exclaimed in frustration: "You are not having the correct difficulties with this exercise. It says right here that you will call opinions facts, but you are all calling facts opinions." This example illustrates one way in which overreliance on tightly coupled prescriptive systems in areas of complex, subtle, intellectual interaction can produce unintended and undesirable results. Another example, on a much larger scale, illustrates the great complexity of the relationship between intentions and actions. Several years ago in California, the statewide board of governors, responding both to public concern and pressure from the leadership of the faculty-led academic senate and from leaders in some discipline-oriented organizations (including the state English council), proposed standards for courses "below the college level," including how many such courses might be applied to the associate degree. In the language developed by the state chancellor's staff, the proposal read "a course one level below Freshman English" could be applied to the degree. This language allowed for any one of many different courses (for example, business English, journalism) at a college to be accepted. In an effort to eliminate this possibility, a group of faculty leaders succeeded in getting the board to adopt a rule that stated "one course a level below Freshman English." Discussion before the board of governors made the intention of this language very clear: each college would be able to designate only one of its remedial courses to qualify for degree credit. And that was the policy adopted by the board. But that isn't what happened in the colleges. Instead, responding to colleges that would be forced to reorganize their English curriculum (an unintended consequence), key people on the state chancellor's staff simply "interpreted" the board's policy to allow for more than one course to be acceptable, dealing with problems raised from individual campuses on a case-by-case basis. Thus, the prescriptive policy was simply modified when it encountered a far more complicated reality than had been contemplated in its development. Here again, an imperfect flow of information between decision-making levels resulted in plans (intentions) that were then expressed in policy. The policy, however, was never implemented as intended. Some might say it was undermined at the point of action, where implementers, working within their own complex realities, behaved in ways inconsistent with the intentions of state policy makers. Another interpretation would hold that the state board attempted to impose a solution based on assumptions of tight coupling for a reality requiring more loosely coupled arrangements.

Recognizing the complexity of acting in institutions, William G. Tierney frames this issue in slightly different terms:

> Even the most seasoned college and university administrators often ask themselves, "What holds this place together? Is it mission, values, bureau-

cratic procedures, or strong personalities? How
does this place run and what does it expect from
its leaders?" These questions usually are asked in
moments of frustration, when seemingly rational,
well-laid plans have failed or have met with unexpected resistance. Similar questions are also asked
frequently by members new to the organization,
persons who want to know "how things are done
around here." Questions like these seem difficult
to answer because there is *no one-to-one corre-
spondence between actions and results* [1988, p. 3;
emphasis added].

Actions That Convey Symbolic Meaning

So far, our discussion has emphasized actions that are codependent: the printing department depends on the administrative offices to provide the copy for the schedule of classes;
the administrative offices in turn depend on the departments
for input; the departments depend on the number of faculty
and rooms available; everyone depends on student interests
and needs. Perhaps one reason that relatively little emphasis
is placed on the *acting* dimension of decision-making processes is its dynamic, ephemeral, codependent nature.

Some acts, however, have intrinsic meaning. This kind
of acting, though it may be part of some larger process, is an
end in itself. And these acts are an important part of organizational life, usually described in the literature as ritual behavior, such as graduation ceremonies, retirement celebrations,
holiday festivities, opening-of-school convocations. These acts
can be quite routine (for example, every Christmas, there is a
party), yet, they have a symbolic dimension that is often more
important than the content of the act itself. Such acts often
have a great impact on organizational climate, which in turn
shapes the context of decision making.

Trustees often play a unique role in such actions. When
we asked in interviews at our study institutions what new ideas
board members had contributed to the college, the responses

invariably related to very tangible actions. At Allan Hancock, a board member arranged for a local service club to replace the unrepairable flagpole; at Santa Monica, a board member suggested fencing for a parking lot that would screen automobile lights from neighboring residences; and at Santa Barbara, a board member donated a new landscaped entrance to the college. At first glance, such actions seem minor, at the margins of the enterprise. But in each case, the new amenities gave physical expression to each college's effort to be a good neighbor, a responsible member of the community. The symbolic meaning of such actions is enormous and should not be underestimated.

The importance of such acts in relation to implementing decisions is underscored by Tierney (1988): "To implement decisions, leaders must have a full, nuanced understanding of the organization's culture. Only then can they articulate decisions in a way that will speak to the needs of various constituencies and marshal their support" (p. 5). Further on, Tierney elaborates: "The president frequently articulates his vision of the institutional mission in his speeches and writing. One individual commented: 'When I first came here and the president said that "we're number one" I just thought it was something he said, like every college president says. But after [you're here] awhile you watch the guy and you see he really believes it. So I believe it too' " (1988, p. 11).

Tierney adds that such presidential pronouncements serve two purposes: to provide rationale and criteria for developing a cohesive curricular program and to establish an institutional standard for self-criticism and performance. In these circumstances, acts of speech and writing are ends in themselves, serving as the occasion for members of the college to bind themselves together, feeling that they are part of an entity greater than a collection of individuals. In this sense, the actions of leaders often differ from those of individuals in the college. If a faculty member writes to the student newspaper expressing views on a proposed parking lot, the letter stands on the merits of its argument. Readers would typically react, "Well, that's one person's view." If the college president or the union president writes to the same newspaper on the same issue, most readers would take the views as having institutional significance. Here the communication carries not only the weight of the individual's argument but also the sense that the position reflects the views of the organization or of an important constituency.

In *The Tasks of Leadership,* John W. Gardner provides a vivid illustration:

> I recall a visit with a young college president who had just come into the job fresh from a professorship, with no prior administrative experience. He confided that he was deeply irked by an incident that had occurred the preceding day. In his first speech before faculty, students, trustees and alumni he had simply been himself—a man of independent mind full of lively personal opinions. Many of his listeners were nonplussed and irritated. They weren't interested in a display of idiosyncratic views. They had expected him to speak as their new leader, their symbol of institutional continuity, their ceremonial collective voice. I told him gently that they had expected him to be their spokesman and symbol, and this simply angered him further. "I'll resign," he said, "if I can't be myself!" Over time, he learned that leaders can rarely afford the luxury of speaking for themselves alone [1986, p. 19].

For this reason, leaders must always evaluate their actions not only according to their personal needs and preferences but also as those actions convey intended meanings to others within the college. That perspective is part of having a "full, nuanced understanding of the organization's culture."

Multiple Realities: The Context of Acting

One useful way of thinking about the meaning of actions in an organization is the analysis of "multiple realities" presented by Bolman and Deal (1984). Every person in the organization experiences a reality different from that experienced by every other person. Every person is, of course, unique. The view of the world from various positions and roles in the organization is also quite different. And each person can interpret most events that occur in the organization from many perspectives. Bolman and Deal describe the four perspectives that Bensimon (1989) used in her analysis of presidential perspectives on leadership.

The *structural* perspective sees organizations as rational instruments created to achieve specific ends. People are deployed in an organizational structure that has been designed to get the organization's job done. The *human resource* point of view focuses on people's needs and objectives that deserve attention by the organization. The *political* frame sees the competition for power and scarce resources as the central activity of organizational life. The *symbolic* perspective asserts that events in organizations have meanings that transcend the occurrences themselves and that these meanings, in some cases, are more important than the events. To give metaphorical life to these frames, Bolman and Deal think of organizations as machines, families, jungles, and theaters. Most actions in organizations will be interpreted in one or more of these terms by various members of the organization.

The young president who saw himself as a man of independent mind full of lively personal opinions was thinking in the human resource domain. He was considering his own needs and was uncomfortable with the constraints of a new job. He had not yet internalized the notion that his behavior conveyed major symbolic meanings within his college community, and we doubt that he was fully aware that he stood at the apex of a complex organizational structure. Soon enough he would also experience the political realities of conflicting interests and limited resources. Developing an understanding of the multiple realities always present in complex organizations and learning to see events from more than one perspective are important tasks for people who wish to provide institutional leadership.

Though we have found less attention to acting in the literature and in our interviews at the study institutions, we believe acting is both critical and complicated. Yet, the deciding process that guides leaders to act or not to act seems as important and integral to governance as the processes of planning and deciding. What we do usually reflects how well we planned and decided.

Chapter Highlights

- The whole point of effective decision making is to produce good outcomes.

- Bolman and Deal (1984, p. 281) state: "An organization that requires everyone to fully justify every course of action before doing anything is likely to be an organization that never does anything new or different. . . . 'Bias for action' becomes a symbol of a culture that supports creativity and risk taking."

- The central action of any community college, the teaching-learning transaction of the classroom and laboratory, is not easily viewed or assessed.

- The real issue may be just which actions in a community college do count and the problem for decision makers becomes determining which actions to count (which can be one of the critical outcomes of a given planning process).

- In any effective organization, the goal is to do the right things right.

- The concepts of tight coupling and loose coupling can guide decision makers who want to do the right things and do things right.

- One of the marks of effective leadership lies in knowing what situations require *reacting*, thereby setting in motion nonroutine decision and communication processes, and which situations require *acting*, merely directing individuals and groups into the usual decision process.

- Evaluation is a distinctive form of acting, one that requires stepping out of the usual flow of events to make judgments and assess outcomes.

- Our observation suggests that even colleges with reasonably effective governance arrangements are more conscious of the processes of planning and deciding than the processes of implementing and evaluating.

- One challenge for leaders, one goal of the governance process, is to find the appropriate mix of tight coupling and loose coupling, the balance between data-based evaluation reports and the direct assessment provided by personal observation.

- Both the compliance approach and the informal monitoring approach can be seen as sensing systems that respond to critical factors, as defined by college officials.

- Some acts have intrinsic meaning, and these acts are an important part of organizational life, usually described in the literature as ritual behavior.

- Leaders must always evaluate their actions not only according to their personal needs and preferences but also as those actions convey intended meanings to others within the college.

- We believe that developing an understanding of the multiple realities always present in complex organizations and learning to see events from more than one perspective are important tasks for persons who wish to provide institutional leadership.

Chapter Six

Reacting

"To every action there is always opposed an equal reaction;
or, the mutual actions of two bodies upon each other
are always equal, and directed to contrary parts."
—Sir Isaac Newton

More than other postsecondary institutions, the community college is a reactive institution. The missions and character of these colleges require sensitive attention to emerging needs and quick response to them. Thus, in some respects the colleges' "clients" create these institutions. In fact, the colleges have developed sensitive mechanisms for discovering what needs reacting to. It is a tribute to the effectiveness of these systems for reacting, for example, that the United States has been able to absorb the enormous influx of Southeast Asians over a span of two decades without creating a new educational infrastructure, in some measure due to the role played by community colleges. However, reacting as an aspect of governance lacks the mathematical certainty of Newton's formulation, requiring a complex set of structures and persons to determine when reacting is necessary and appropriate.

Sensing Mechanisms

Just how the community college has developed mechanisms and systems for reacting is not entirely clear. But we can identify a number of features—both structural and personal—that keep the institution in close touch with its communities and constituencies. In states where college trustees are popularly elected, the political process establishes an awareness of and sensitivity to community needs and concerns. Even in states

103

where trustees are appointed (for example, Florida), a major role of the board of trustees is to reflect community perceptions to the college leadership, a role explicitly identified both by trustees and by the president of Jefferson Community College. Public trustee meetings with agendas allowing citizens to speak in open forum provide another mechanism for sensing community issues.

When community colleges establish new curricula and new programs, advisory boards of business and community leaders are a common feature. From time to time, most colleges conduct surveys and needs assessments among students or parts of the community. Perhaps just as important as these structural elements, community colleges have long encouraged an entrepreneurial spirit among staff and faculty. Since most faculty and staff live among the students and citizens they serve, they see and hear the concerns of friends, neighbors, and other associates. Many participate in community organizations, such as Rotary, Kiwanis, Lions, American Association of University Women, League of Women Voters, Parent-Teacher Association, Young Men's Christian Association, and Young Women's Christian Association as well as youth sports, scouting, and recreational activities. George Vaughan's research on the community college presidency revealed that "86 percent of the presidents belong to one or more service clubs," with Rotary International alone enrolling 65 percent of the presidents (1986, p. 24). Because the community college has come to perceive the community as its campus, it is quick to respond to needs defined by knowledgeable staff and faculty and is quite ready to take programs and courses to the people when that is the most effective way to serve them.

The Meaning of Reacting

Acknowledging the reactive character of the community college, we want to clarify that our use of the term *reacting* is limited and focused. As we noted in Chapter Five, we distinguish *reacting* from *deciding* and *acting* because it allows us to examine important differences in the overall process of decision making. Thus, as we use the terms, *acting* relates to the ordinary day-to-day processes and predictable activities that occur in community colleges both before and after *deciding*. *Reacting*, on the other hand, applies to the nonordinary, unpredictable situations that occur, require response, and either set in motion processes for deciding or flow from them. A key to this distinction lies in recognizing those features of an event or situation that demand reacting. To some extent, decision makers can establish systems to monitor routine events (such as enrollment patterns, faculty load, cash flow) so that an unexpected change in pattern can be noted and reacted to. But in many cases, the sensor lies within key persons in the organization. On October 17, 1989, when the Loma Prieta earthquake struck northern California, three administrators were on duty at De Anza College. Although the shake was considerable and power went out, the initial conversation between two of the administrators (both with considerable experience in California) was how the quake compared to others. No crisis was perceived. But a few minutes later, the third administrator, responsible for evening college, heard a radio report that a portion of the Bay Bridge had collapsed. That key piece of information redefined the situation for her. She immediately made the decision to close the campus before darkness fell.

At Jefferson Community College in Kentucky, several interviews turned up a commonly perceived crisis: the governor's budget of the previous year contained no increases for higher education. Institutional reactions took many forms: President Ronald Horvath set about gaining increased information from the system chancellor to determine how this would affect his college's budget. He took pains to involve as many members of his staff and faculty as possible. The business manager described the process for developing contingency budget cuts at intervals of 1 percent, 2 percent, 3 percent, and so on. Both groups of faculty interviewed referred to the special meetings and discussions on budget cuts. One group also mentioned another form of reaction: political activity to lobby the legislature, which involved forming an organization of business people called Advocates for Higher Education and holding rallies in the state capital involving students, bands, and selected leaders speaking to the governor.

Another situation that required reacting was mentioned in practically every interview at Santa Monica College—a parking crisis. Following is a synopsis of how two senior administrators described the problem: "The college has 1200 to 1300 on-campus parking spaces, but as many as 5000 students park at peak times. The overflow parks in surrounding neighborhoods (where over the past several years home values have risen from $50,000 to $350,000). Residents, unhappy with the congestion, noise, litter, and occasional student making a U-turn on someone's lawn, go to the City Council and get the area designated for preferential parking (no students during specified hours, beginning six months later). In response, the college begins to plan a parking structure, but neighborhood groups object to various proposed placements." Since President Richard Moore perceived this issue as one that could have long-term impact on the college, limiting growth or perhaps even forcing reduced enrollments, he reacted with several simultaneous initiatives: a joint special committee was formed including college trustees and city council members; reports were made by President Moore weekly to the Three Presidents group, less frequently to the whole faculty senate; staff resources were redirected in order to establish a parking task force and to reassign an administrator to coordinate the college's activities; consultants were hired; special communications—both oral and written—were developed to educate the entire college community on the situation; and special efforts were undertaken in the state legislature to increase the maximum parking fee students could be charged as a means to finance the needed parking garage.

Another kind of crisis was described by senior staff at Miami-Dade: about ten o'clock one evening, a report was received that $15,000 was missing from bookstore receipts. A police report was filed, but the event also required prompt notification of the college president, the trustees, and other key college leaders, mainly so no one would be surprised by press articles from the police investigation. A reaction after the immediate crisis was a review of the cash-handling and auditing procedures employed in various areas of the college operation. Those we interviewed did not feel that special decision processes were necessary in this case but that more intense use of existing channels and procedures was required, such as phone calls at unusual hours and special meetings of existing groups. This crisis was not seen as one posing long-term consequences for the college.

Routine Versus Critical Decisions

To place college officials' reactions to ordinary as opposed to crisis decisions in an appropriate context, we find Selznick's (1957) distinction between routine and critical decisions useful. Routine decisions have to do with the maintenance and operation of the organization, the important everyday decisions required to ensure, for example, that students are registered for classes, proper controls exist for handling money, student and employee safety procedures are in place and practiced, buildings are lighted and heated, the payroll is generated accurately and on time, and so on. These decisions are required for the proper management of the organization, but essential as they are, they do not significantly change the nature or the character of the institution. When, for example, public agencies were required by federal law in 1987 to implement the Consolidated Omnibus Budget Reconciliation Act (COBRA) program under which former employees could continue to purchase medical benefits for up to thirty-six months, the administrative decisions required to comply with the federal mandate were complex and costly, but the affected organizations were not changed in any fundamental way. The required adaptations were essentially static rather than dynamic.

Selznick contrasts such matters of routine activity with the area of critical experience: "There is a vital sector of organizational experience that cannot be understood as simple problem-solving in which the organization remains essentially intact. Rather, in this sector we find such adaptations of leadership to the interplay of internal and external forces as result in basic institutional changes. This is the area of 'character-defining' commitments, which affect the organization's capacity to control its own future behavior" (1957, pp. 35–37).

Two examples of such "character-defining" commitments can be found in the consequences of California's Proposition 13 in 1978. This measure constituted a revolt against the ad valorem property tax, a system that in some respects had become confiscatory, given the runaway escalation of property values in the state. Prior to 1978, California community college districts had been permitted under the law to levy a tax of up to five cents per one hundred dollars of assessed valuation to provide community services in the local area. Services funded by this tax included noncredit short-course programs, concert and lecture series, off-campus community outreach centers, and use of college facilities by community groups, among others. College districts levying this tax paid their community service staffs from its proceeds rather than from district general funds.

Proposition 13 amended the state constitution to eliminate this tax and others like it. Critical decisions were then required concerning what to do with community service staffs in those districts that had significant numbers of people paid from the funds that had been eliminated. In order to protect their general fund resources, a number of districts laid off their community service staffs en masse. One notable community college district, in contrast, transferred the entire group onto its general fund, thus beginning a pattern of actions that contributed eventually to a form of district bankruptcy, the necessity to request an emergency bailout loan from the state, the imposition by the state legislature of stringent fiscal controls, and the placement of a state monitor in the district. The critical decision in this district not to reduce or eliminate its community service staff did, in fact, constitute a commitment that affected the organization's capacity to control its own future behavior.

Similarly, in the aftermath of Proposition 13, the state legislature passed an emergency one-year "block grant" funding statute. Unlike previous funding measures, this law was not enrollment driven. Districts received the same amount of money regardless of whether their enrollment went down or up. As a consequence, to save money, some districts canceled their summer sessions and cut back course offerings they had planned to provide during the academic year. Other districts continued to provide services to the fullest extent possible. These, too, were critical decisions that affected the colleges' capacity to control their own future behavior. The following year the legislature returned to a work load–driven funding formula. The districts that had maintained their momentum and their educational programs fared better than those that had curtailed theirs.

One of the crucial tasks of leaders is to distinguish between routine incidents and critical events and to behave appropriately to each. The distinction was suggested by a CEO who had been called out of a meeting to take an "emergency" telephone call. When he returned, he described the matter as "urgent but not important." Though the loss of electricity on campus as night falls is an urgent matter when one must decide whether to cancel evening classes, it is not important in the sense that the nature of the educational program will be shaped by the decision. Such an event does not pose a threat to the character or long-term health of the college and does not require extensive reacting. As we mentioned in Chapter Five, the institution, or the official, who overreacts to minor, if urgent, issues risks the waste of vital energy and attention on trivial problems. President Jimmy Carter's attempt to resolve interpersonal conflict on his staff over the use of the White House tennis court by personally preparing the schedule for the court comes to mind as an example. On the other hand, the institution that treats an important new event, some happening that is fundamentally different, as though it were merely another routine occurrence invites disaster. Nowhere in higher education was this more evident than in the case of the University of California, Berkeley, in the 1960s.

In the early fall of 1964, students at the University of California, Berkeley, were actively supporting William Scranton's opposition to the nomination of Barry Goldwater at the Republican National Convention in San Francisco. They organized convention rallies and demonstrations from tables set up outside Sather Gate on the Berkeley campus. The campus administration judged these activities to be in violation of campus rules and ordered the tables removed. This action ignited an inferno of disruptive activity, the sparks from which spread across much of American higher education. Before the Berkeley Free Speech Movement had run its course, campus operations had been brought virtually to a halt, the chancellor and other senior officials of the Berkeley administration had lost their jobs, Ronald Reagan had won the governorship of the state on a platform of restoring order to the university, and shortly after Reagan's election as governor, the president of the university, Clark Kerr, was removed from office.

One leader of the Free Speech Movement, Mario Savio, a student in the Berkeley philosophy department, provides some insight into the need for appropriate reaction in his protest speech titled "An End to History":

> In our free-speech fight at the University of California, we have come up against what may emerge as the greatest problem of our nation—depersonalized, unresponsive bureaucracy. We have encountered the organized status quo in Mississippi, but it is the same in Berkeley. Here we find it impossible usually to meet with anyone but secretaries. Beyond that, we find functionaries who cannot make policy but can only hide behind the rules. We have discovered total lack of response on the part of policy makers. To grasp a situation which is truly Kafkaesque, it is necessary to understand the bureaucratic mentality. . . .
>
> As bureaucrat, an administrator believes that nothing new happens. He occupies an a-

historical point of view. In September, to get the attention of this bureaucracy . . . we held a sit-in on the campus. . . . At last, the administrative bureaucracy agreed to negotiate. But instead, on the following Monday, we discovered that a committee had been appointed, in accordance with usual regulations, to resolve the dispute. *Our attempt to convince any of the administrators that an event had occurred, that something new had happened, failed. They saw this simply as something to be handled by normal university procedures* [Lipset and Wolin, 1965, p. 216; emphasis added].

Recognizing the Critical Event

No doubt, if the Berkeley administrators could have gained even a fleeting glimpse of the consequences of their actions, they would have behaved quite differently. But it is not always possible, certainly at the onset, to know when something genuinely new has occurred or to know that one has handled it badly. Also, it is not always possible to know the magnitude of the forces with which one is dealing in the early stages of an emerging situation. As Henry Kissinger has observed of complex issues in international relations, when one's scope of action is at the maximum, one's information is usually at the minimum. By the time one's information is at the maximum, one's scope of action has been reduced to the minimum. Nevertheless, it is a key task of those in positions of responsibility to sense when an important new circumstance has arisen and to respond appropriately. Going back to the examples at the beginning of the chapter, in our view, President Horvath at Jefferson College and President Moore at Santa Monica correctly perceived the threat to their institutions (one in actual reductions in dollars, the other in potential loss of a large number of students) and designed strategies for reacting appropriate to the circumstance.

One can, as Selznick observes, make a series of critical,

character-defining decisions without being aware that one is doing so (1957, p. 44). Perhaps the district that transferred its community service staff onto its general fund was not aware of the critical nature of that decision. Thus, no decision (that is, not reacting) in the face of a critical event can also constitute a character-defining choice.

Community colleges, given changing economic and demographic conditions and the flow of political events in local communities, always run the risk of presuming that what has worked in the past for the institution will continue to work in the future. As Birnbaum observes of People's Community College, "The very programs created by People's to enable it to repeat its successes ironically may inhibit its perception of new problems" (1988, p. 118). The "nothing fails like success" paradox is discussed by Kouzes and Posner in *The Leadership Challenge*. Citing research on innovation, they note that "success does not breed success. It breeds failure. It is failure which breeds success" (1987, p. 63). Foothill-De Anza's shared governance process, embodied in its Budget and Policy Development Group, as we observed in Chapter Four, grew directly from a crisis in trust, a situation of impasse in negotiations that went to mediation and fact finding. Though the immediate situation was resolved, all parties to the process—board, administration, faculty—regarded it as a failure. That failure motivated the effort to create a new process.

Abandoning purposes that are vital to institutional existence can also be life threatening. As we noted in Chapter Two, junior colleges were created essentially to serve functions of transfer and occupational education for young people. In the decades of the 1960s and 1970s, junior colleges successfully diversified their mission and expanded their programs in order to respond to rapid social changes and emerging community needs. In some community colleges these processes of rapid diversification caused the educational focus, particularly on transfer education, to become blurred. This led to major criticisms of the institution, and in some quarters to a belief that community colleges had developed a diminished capacity to serve the transfer function. To the extent that such a condition were permitted to develop, it would certainly be character changing.

The Role of Experience and Information

For leaders trying to determine what is critical and what is routine, when to react and when to act, experience and information are two of the most useful aids for gauging what is important. Both have significant limitations. Experience is an indispensable guide to the administrator in trying to understand that which is critical within the flow of institutional events. Experience incorporates both one's sense of institutional history and one's knowledge of what has succeeded in the past. But experience alone can be misleading. As Tom Fryer has observed,

> In administration experience provides the key understandings of what is likely to work and what is not, where things are likely to come loose and where they are secure, under what conditions people are likely to accept a decision or will be antagonized by it or reject it, and so on. Experience teaches the subtleties, inflections, and complexities of the institutional context without which truly effective administration is impossible.
>
> The paradox derives from the fact that however broad one's experience, considering the total universe, one's personal sample is extremely small, and is possibly quite unrepresentative either of the universe or of the next circumstance in which one finds himself [Fryer, 1982, pp. 10–11].

Information must also play a role in handling critical events or crises. At Santa Barbara City College, the hotel and restaurant management program expanded to include a 110-room hotel, a restaurant, and food service for an 800-person retirement community. The possibility for a major crisis became apparent when it was clear to the college president and the board of trustees that the program was overextended, with not enough students to handle all the operations. Further complicating the situation was the financial risk these operations posed to the entire college and the potential litigation from local unions who saw their members being displaced from jobs. In such a complex situation, getting information to key people (in this case the president, board members, and three senior administrators) to provide the basis for problem definition was crucial. At the outset, Santa Barbara President Peter McDougall confined discussions to board members and top management. Since litigation was one aspect of the situation, the board met as a committee of the whole in intensive sessions, thus ensuring that all critical decision makers would be working from a common base of information. This procedure also provided the opportunity for any differences among these key people to be worked out before matters were broached for public discussion. Once the leadership had formulated the issues, information was disseminated through the organization and other elements of the college could react through the usual channels of communication. At Mt. San Antonio College, a board member emphasized the importance of a system of communication between board members and President Jack Randall, especially for situations that could bring unwarranted negative attention to the college. This board member recalled being contacted by Randall at a Girl Scout cookout on a Sunday morning about a potentially damaging incident. Despite the inconvenience, he was pleased to have gotten immediate notification of the situation.

Good information always seems scarce in crises. As we noted in Chapter Four, this fact encourages leaders to create large-scale, complex information systems, which require enormous resources to design, install, and maintain. Such systems are so resource intensive that, as Birnbaum observes of People's information system, "Processes initially set up to support goals may become goals in themselves; perpetuating the means may become the ends" (1988, p. 117). It is also possible that the data so necessary for the efficient management of the organization in the middle levels can create a condition called "trained incapacity" at the highest levels. Selznick observes, "The logic of efficiency loses force . . . as we approach the top of the pyramid. Problems at this level are more resistant to the ordinary approach of management experts. Mechanical metaphors—the organization as a 'smooth running machine'—suggest an overemphasis on neat organization and on efficient techniques of administration. It is probable that these emphases induce in the analyst a trained incapacity to observe the interrelation of policy and administration, with the result that the really critical experience of organizational leadership is largely overlooked" (1957, p. 3).

Trust, mutual respect, and credibility are qualities that must be fostered at all times among organizational leaders. In times of crisis, those qualities prove essential. When information is uncertain and conflicting versions of events are put forward both within the organization and before the public, decision makers must rely on the openness and integrity of key people. Where there is trust, people will give each other the benefit of the doubt, allowing one another to focus on the problem at hand, rather than argue personalities or question motives.

The subject of our discussion in this chapter is the unusual events that are as unpredictable as they are inevitable in the course of organization life. As we have seen, these events can be either routine or critical. Of course, "routine" does not necessarily mean "minor." When asbestos was discovered during the process of reinforcing the Wheeler Hall structure on the Berkeley campus to resist earthquakes, the building had to be closed. This crisis during 1988–1989 was anything but minor. The entire English department had to be relocated for over a year, dozens of class sections had to be moved on an already overcrowded campus, the financial cost of the asbestos removal was enormous. When the main electrical switch bringing electricity into the De Anza College campus exploded in March 1989, leaving the campus and much of the surrounding neighborhood without power, the resulting situation was certainly not minor. For a time it was thought that all the current Foothill-De Anza District's student record files had been lost when the mainframe computer crashed as a result of the power failure. Such events are thoroughly nonroutine in the everyday sense of that word. But they are quite routine in the important way that Selznick uses the term: neither problem nor solution changed the character of the University of California, Berkeley, or the Foothill-De Anza Community College District in any fundamental way.

Unusual situations can arise internally in institutions or be the result of external events. Media "exposés" are one form of externally produced crisis, as when a major daily newspaper a number of years ago ran a story concerning a graduate of the local community college who could neither read nor write. They can also be created internally as when a highly respected, senior faculty member writes an open letter to his colleagues alleging that the institution's affirmative action program is failing miserably, or when the college president, as a result of the news story on the illiterate graduate, launches a major reform initiative in the institution. Whatever the particulars of the event requiring reacting, responsible people must determine whether the event is critical or routine. Where the event is judged critical, efforts must be made to define accurately the issues involved, to develop procedures for managing misinformation in the college and the community (rumors and gossip are powerful forces in a crisis), and to devise a plan for keeping all key decision makers informed as the reactions to the critical event develop and unfold. Some of the techniques employed by those we interviewed included much more intensive communication (daily between president and board, even more frequently between president and key leaders in the college); special meetings of regularly constituted governance groups, including the board, administrative groups, faculty senates and unions; and creation of ad hoc groups that cut across the usual governance groupings (for example, the Santa Monica Parking Task

Force and the joint committee of trustees and city council members). In all of this, the overriding goal is to give the crisis the full attention and resources it requires so that, as quickly as feasible, the institution can return to its normal decision-making processes, acting rather than reacting. Because a crisis requires much more intensive communicating than ordinary circumstances, it often tests the quality of communication within an organization. Just what constitutes high-quality communication is the subject of our next chapter.

Chapter Highlights

• More than other postsecondary institutions, the community college is a reactive institution.

• Acknowledging the reactive character of the community college, we limit our use of the term *reacting* to apply to the nonordinary, unpredictable situations that occur, require response, and either set in motion processes for *deciding* or flow from them.

• We find Selznick's (1957) distinction between routine and critical decisions useful. Routine decisions have to do with the maintenance and operation of the organization—important everyday decisions. Critical decisions are those "character-defining" commitments that affect the organization's capacity to control its own future behavior.

• One of the crucial tasks of responsible officials is to distinguish between routine events and critical incidents and to behave appropriately to each.

• When a critical event occurs but is not reacted to for what it is, the results can affect the institution's capacity to control its own future.

• Community colleges, given changing economic and demographic conditions and the flow of political events in local communities, always run the risk of presuming that what has worked in the past will continue to work in the future.

• Abandoning functions that are vital to basic institutional purposes can threaten the institution's future.

• For leaders trying to determine what is critical and what is routine, when to react and when to act, experience and information, in spite of their limitations, are two of the most useful aids for gauging what is important among institutional events.

• In all of this, the overriding goal is to give the crisis the attention and resources it requires so that, as quickly as feasible, the institution can return to its normal decision-making processes, acting rather than reacting.

Chapter Seven

Communicating

"Good, the more
Communicated, more abundant grows."
—John Milton

A committee in a community college has been wrangling for forty-five minutes about exactly what a decision made by the president's cabinet means and how it should be implemented. The feeling level in the group is high and tempers have begun to flare. At this moment, one participant suddenly glows with insight and announces, with considerable feeling: "The problem we have here is one of communication!" This little scenario has become a cliché of modern organizational discourse. The analysis is accurate, but not very helpful. Clearly, communication is a critical element of the process leading to a decision and of the process implementing a decision. But simply noting that fact does not help decision makers and decision implementers assess the effectiveness of communication in the organization. This chapter will present several ways of thinking about communication processes related to decision making in community colleges by introducing some key concepts of good organizational communication and by describing several examples of successful communication processes. To set the stage for this discussion, we will first sketch a scenario in a community college that demonstrates the problematic nature of communicating in complex organizations.

Two pertinent values have been communicated throughout this community college district: (1) participation in decision making should occur at all levels of the colleges, involving all categories of staff—administrators, faculty, and

120

classified; (2) materials that go to the board of trustees must meet a high standard of clarity and correctness. The district CEO tries to model both of these values in the decision structures he uses to prepare recommendations for the board. On occasion, when materials for board actions sent from College A have not met this standard, they have been returned to the responsible college administrator with sharply worded notes about the deficiencies in the written materials. One effect of this procedure has been to heighten the sensitivity of campus administrators to the quality of material destined for review by the board of trustees. But as messages get transmitted through many levels by many different individuals, much of the nuance and subtlety of the original communication is lost. In one vivid case, efforts to adhere to an important organizational value resulted, paradoxically, in undermining that value.

The district had just adopted a new set of tenure review guidelines. Each campus had developed its own new procedures for carrying out the tenure review process within those guidelines. Because a great number of new faculty had been hired that year, a significant number of tenured staff were serving on tenure review committees. The procedures were new and all members of the committees needed to learn the new requirements. And, of course, the reports produced by the committees would all go to the board of trustees for review and action.

To complicate this particular situation, the faculty member coordinating the process was relatively new to the organization and was not well known among more senior faculty. In addition, a staff assistant was hired, in part, to manage the enormous paper flow that the new system would generate. Under the circumstances, some failed communications are not surprising. One resulting problem was fairly typical and easily correctable; the other was more unusual.

All tenure review committee members attended a workshop on the new process. Among the materials provided at the workshop was a time line indicating when each step of the process would be completed. One line stated: "Nov. 17—

Student evaluations completed and turned in." However, student evaluations were not discussed in the workshop. Two weeks later, each tenure committee chair was sent a memo outlining "Duties of Committee Chairs." One item read: "4. Administer the student evaluation (or if you are not administering it yourself, see that it is completed by November 17)." Most committee chairs did not understand that they were responsible for conducting student evaluations. This was a new element of the procedure, one that was never communicated in the workshop. Only the memo quoted above conveyed this expectation. Though many people did not get the message, the problem was easily remedied. A clarifying memo was sent to each committee chair and the tenure review coordinator left a message in the voice mail system for each chair.

Because she had been the unhappy recipient of marked-up material returned from the district CEO, the dean who supervised the new staff assistant underscored the importance of having all the faculty evaluations clear and correct. In an effort to carry out this important task, the staff assistant sent the following memo:

> TO: All Tenure Review Committee Members +
> All Division Secretaries
> FROM: Staff Assistant
> RE: Tenure Review Faculty Evaluation Format—
> VERY IMPORTANT INSTRUCTIONS
> As the tenure coordinator has told you in previous memos, I am responsible for assisting with the administration of the Tenure Review process. Consequently I have the rather delicate task of reviewing all faculty evaluations for form and content. This is not a particularly easy job; as you know, any materials presented to the Board for review must be completely accurate in all respects. Therefore, **ANY EVALUATION CONTAINING ERRORS OF ANY KIND** (including grammar, spelling, punctuation, and/or *spacination*) **WILL BE RETURNED TO THE**

AUTHOR FOR CORRECTION. It's a dirty job, but somebody's got to do it.

While I'm in the mood, let me bring up one last point of importance in getting your review approved. This year we have slightly modified the acceptable format for tenure review write-ups; this has been done in an effort to provide consistency. **ALL REVIEWS ARE TO BE PRINTED ON WHITE PAPER. THE APPROPRIATE COVER SHEET** (pink for faculty evaluations of faculty, buff for administrative evaluation of faculty) **MUST BE SIGNED AND INCLUDED AS THE FIRST PAGE OF THE EVALUATION PACKAGE. . . . PLEASE DO IT RIGHT!**

Not surprisingly, many faculty were upset by this memo. Most of them had never met and many had never heard of the person who sent the memo. The author did not review the memo with anyone before sending it. He believed he was responding to important directions from his supervisors but failed to consider how readers would receive his memo. Senior faculty were outraged to learn that their evaluations would be reviewed for form and *content* by someone who had no faculty or administrative status. One faculty member went so far as to resign from a tenure review committee as a result of the memo.

Perhaps most pertinent to a discussion of communicating in organizations, we can note that the memo's author had significantly misread his audience. Beyond that, he had adopted a tone that was likely to get exactly the opposite response of the one intended. One of the difficulties in remedying such a situation is that a memo like this develops a life of its own. Within a few weeks, copies were circulating informally among faculty at another college in the district. The negative, unintended effects of a badly conceived and/or badly executed written communication can be significant, often undoing good work or requiring extensive time and energy to respond to those upset by the communication. In the worst case, material published by the college (such as cutesy course titles or jargon-ridden course descriptions) can be picked up by the local press and held up to ridicule. We give this point such emphasis because even a well-designed decision-making process can founder on the shoals of bad communication.

As part of its system of internal governance, every community college must establish regular structures and processes for communication. Although ad hoc structures and processes are occasionally necessary for special circumstances, a regular, predictable, well-understood communication structure is essential to create a sense of trust and credibility among members of the organization. We found a wide variety of structures in the districts we studied, yet they all shared these features: redundancy, multiple channels, clarity, and credibility. Each was made to function through effort, commitment, and a kind of institutionalized mutual respect that was reflected in what we call the "no-surprises" rule.

Redundancy

Redundancy may seem a curious feature to find desirable. Most of us realize that in a memo, report, paper, or other document, redundancy is undesirable. Good writers and good editors remove redundancies. But communicating in an organization requires a more complex conception.

We can illustrate by considering two situations. The first involves a commonplace issue in communication. A policy decision has been made by the board of trustees to modify college attendance accounting procedures. This change involves every faculty member, all members of the registrar's staff, and a number of other staff involved in record keeping and reporting. In order to reach everyone involved, the message must be repeated and it must appear in more than one place. In order to make this happen, key communicators in the organization will both hear and repeat the policy changes several times.

The second situation is less traditional. In this particular college, the board, the administration, and the faculty have committed themselves to shared decision making. Such a process depends on the shared belief of all parties that communication is open and honest, that all important information related to a decision has been made available. That process also requires that such information be provided *before* the decision is made. To ensure that information reaches all parts of the organization, repetitive and redundant communications must be employed.

Jefferson Community College presented an excellent model of the redundancy principle. President Ronald Horvath meets weekly with what is called at Jefferson the "8 Group," consisting of deans from both campuses of the college and the budget director. On alternate weeks, he holds administrative staff meetings. These include the deans from the "8 Group," but also include division chairs, some program heads, and mid-managers from nonacademic areas. These meetings serve primarily for information exchange. Once a month, each campus holds an academic staff meeting and student services staff meeting. Once a month, the faculty council meets. The council is presided over by Horvath as the college president, but its membership is faculty members elected from each campus. A faculty vice-chair is elected from each campus. This group is another forum for information exchange, but it also sets the agenda for issues to be acted on at faculty meetings.

Completing the ever-widening circle of communication, a meeting of the entire campus faculty is held each month (three times a year the faculties of the two campuses meet jointly). Certain issues of academic policy are voted on at these faculty meetings. But they also provide another forum for information exchange. Horvath noted that some people will hear the same report as many as four times—clear redundancy—but those people also become knowledgeable communicators within the organization.

We found another example of the redundancy principle operating in a memorandum (dated April 14, 1988) from

Robert McCabe, President of Miami-Dade College, to "Faculty and Professional Staff" regarding one aspect of the Teaching-Learning Project we discussed in Chapter Three:

> I am pleased to share with you this report from the faculty Excellence Subcommittee of the Teaching/Learning Project. You are holding the third draft. Draft #1 was developed primarily from your responses to a survey circulated during October 1987. Draft #2, revised after a Teaching/Learning Project Steering Committee review was thoroughly critiqued at a retreat in March 1988 attended by over 70 of your M-DCC colleagues and outside consultants; Draft #3 emerged from that session.
>
> In the fall of 1988, you will be formally asked for a reaction to this document. I am circulating it now because I believe its contents are important enough to warrant considerable time for study. A clear and agreed upon definition of faculty excellence at M-DCC is necessary as a basis to proceed with the next critical phases of our Teaching/Learning Project. Your participation in the process is essential.

Such redundancy also enhances trust by reinforcing the sense that all groups are receiving the same message as opposed, for example, to the faculty receiving one body of information and the administration a somewhat different version. This approach demands considerable effort in time, energy, and commitment, qualities we discuss more fully later in this chapter.

Multiple Channels

Beyond redundancy, communication about a policy decision that is being formulated or as it is being implemented must be multichannel—"channel" being the mode of communication: speech, print, or electronic. We know that students have preferred learning styles—some more visual, others more auditory; those who work in community colleges have similar preferred channels for receiving and attending to information. The problem from an organizational perspective is that planners and decision makers do not know which channels are preferred by which employees. Thus, when a message is important enough that it must reach all parts of the organization, it should be presented in print (by memo, in-house publications, posters and signs), in speech (at regular meetings, specially called meetings, informal contacts), and electronically (voice mail, electronic mail, closed circuit television, telephone trees).

In an academic department at one of the study districts, a mild controversy developed over the issue of offering an existing course in a television format. Several faculty who objected to the offering based part of their objections on their perception that the faculty had not been consulted before the department head decided to offer the course. The department head produced minutes summarizing discussion of the issue at two separate meetings. The minutes had been distributed to all faculty. Yet, a number of faculty claimed they had never heard of the proposal. Some of the objecting faculty had only read the minutes and others had only attended the meeting; the department head theorized that those who attended the meeting were print channel types and those who read the minutes were speech channel types.

At Mt. San Antonio College in Walnut, California, Acting President Joseph Zagorski described several of the methods his institution uses for communicating on policy issues. Board agendas and all backup materials for the agenda are circulated throughout the management staff and to leaders of faculty, classified staff, and students. All departments and committees are required to publish minutes, which are circulated to key managers. The college president holds a weekly meeting with the academic senate president and with the faculty association president. He also holds open "cookies and milk" sessions, allowing any faculty member to drop in to ask questions or raise concerns. Each month a different trustee holds an office hour on campus to speak with and hear from staff members. One effect of this multichannel approach to communication was reports from all elements of the college that decision makers were open and accessible.

At Miami-Dade, as in other study institutions, the campuses and the district office are linked by a voice-mail system, an electronic channel for communicating that permits nonsimultaneous conversations to occur and the transmission of one message to lists of relevant people. It also allows individuals to be notified of a more substantial communication that will come in a memo or at a meeting. Because this telephone system is at work twenty-four hours a day, seven days a week, senders and receivers of messages do not have to be available at the same time or during normal working hours. This system does not replace print or speech, but adds a third channel to help increase the accuracy and the timeliness of organizational communications.

Clarity

Elsewhere in this book we have spoken of the ambiguity inherent in modern, complex organizations. Ambiguity grows out of the simple reality that communicating any decision cannot be instantaneous and universal. Some employees know more than others. Some learn of decisions before others. Some pay less attention to institutionwide issues than others. Monroe Community College observed this phenomenon during its strategic planning work: "Decision-makers generalized from past experiences and made unexamined assumptions for current decisions. In some cases this led to accepting as *fait accomplis* rigidities that could be changed—or maybe already had been changed." Thus, at any given moment, some part of the organization is acting under the old form of a just-changed policy while other parts implement the new form of that policy. On occasion, two employees, both convinced they know college policy, one aware of a change, the other not, will argue vigorously the rightness of their positions. Often the same word means different things to different people. The simple noun *fund,* for example, has special meanings to accountants that it does not have for others.

Given the inevitability of such ambiguities, pains must be taken to make communications as clear and precise as possible. A poorly written memo, a garbled phone message, or a confused presentation simply adds uncertainty to ambiguity. The result can be expensive in both wasted time and unnecessary frustration. But clarity is important not only in the substance of a communication. Members of the organization should know whom to communicate with about a particular decision. In the districts we studied, even when individuals did not favor some aspect of the existing decision-making process, they expressed a clear understanding of what that process was. They knew the routes in the organization that a budget decision, or a personnel decision, or a new idea would have to travel.

At Santa Monica College, virtually every respondent—trustee, manager, faculty member, classified staff, student leader—reported that if someone wanted to implement a new idea, that person needed to get to Superintendent-President Richard Moore for support. The decision-making channel was clear throughout the organization. At another college, one faculty member observed that changes occurred only with the support of the president. For that reason, he would contrive to encounter the president at the water fountain outside the president's office to try out his new idea. If the president seemed open to the idea, he would then take it through the formal decision process. Again, the process was clearly understood.

Credibility and Trustworthiness

Associated with clarity is credibility. Information must not only be understandable, but must also originate from a trustworthy source. Nowhere is this more important than in budget decision processes. Obviously, budget-related information must be reliable and accurate. No matter how many data are provided in the form of printouts or account ledgers, members of the organization must believe that critical information is not being held back, that there is no hidden process where the "true" facts are presented and the "real" decisions made. Many community colleges promote widespread participation on the input side of the budget process, asking individuals and departments to make requests for their needs (frequently referred to as "wish lists" in districts we studied). Yet, some of these same colleges make the critical decisions to allocate resources in a small group of senior administrators where the values and facts that count in setting priorities may be out of the view of most members of the institution. Such colleges run the risk of "funnel vision." Most of the inner surface of a funnel is open to easy inspection, but it narrows dramatically at the end where the "final allocation" is made. If the decisions that emerge from the narrow, closed end of the funnel do not reflect the information and values that were contributed in the open end of the funnel, then the credibility of the whole process is at risk.

The Foothill-De Anza Community College District has established a budget process that opens up the narrow end of the funnel. Not only are budget processes broadly participated in at the division and campus level, but the critical allocation alternatives, both for revenue and expenditures, are considered openly in the District Budget and Policy Development Group (BPDG). The chancellor decides what recommendations to take to the board of trustees on the basis of presentations and discussions at the BPDG, which includes the leaders of all employee organizations, including unions, as well as key members of the campus and district management staffs. If the priorities of a particular department or even an entire campus are not agreed to, the leaders who represent the members of those entities are present and participate in the discussions that lead to such a decision. In his monograph "Collaborative Governance in the Foothill/De Anza Community College District," Cyril Gulassa observes: "The BPDG stresses visibility. At any point where the decision-making process stream flows underground, out of the view of the other parties, bad things begin to happen, and these bad things include cynicism, paranoia and distrustfulness. In the BPDG, all decisions are made at the table, in full view of all participants. Everyone not only understands how decisions are made, they witness *how* and *what* others think and perceive underlying values, which leads to mutual respect and, to a degree, even affection" (1989, pp. 3-4). Thus, there is no place in the structure of the organization where communications related to decision making disappear from the view of interested parties or their representatives.

Effort and Commitment

Clear, credible, multichannel communication obviously does not happen by accident. Whatever structures or processes a particular college has established, key members of the organization work very hard to keep them functioning effectively. One district chancellor observed that "our structure is methodical and laborious—it takes time." A faculty member in another district described his college's planning and budgeting process as "a black hole in terms of time." In fact, when we asked respondents in one study what weaknesses they saw in their decision processes, the most common response referred to the amount of time required. Though "taking a lot of time" was often reported as a negative, organizations that get their members to give their time have real evidence of commitment—the upside of this expenditure of time. Although recognizing this cost in time, President Peter Spina still committed Monroe Community College to a long-term effort, as his planners describe vividly: "Strategic planning at MCC has developed in ways that are uniquely ours, shaped by our temperament and environment. The process may be taking longer than we might wish, especially those of us who long for seven-day creations, but patience becomes us—even if it is a piercing virtue." At Miami-Dade Community College, a board member observed: "There's a mystique about this college that encourages professors to teach here even though money might be better somewhere else." At the same college, a senior faculty member echoed that notion of commitment: "To be part of something great, you have to give up more."

At Allan Hancock College, President Gary Edelbrock noted a long tradition of faculty participation in decision making about curriculum and hiring. We found evidence of much effort on the part of faculty as well as management to make these decision processes work. Many respondents spoke of the college as a family. And one commented: "The college really does work like a family. You have some children who don't do their chores." Thus, the importance of effort and commitment can be documented in their absence as well. Members of the institution take note when others do not do their share. One of the most difficult issues raised by effective communication processes (which inevitably require much effort and energy) is one of fairness: finding ways of equitably and fairly distributing the work among members of the institution was a problem noted in every one of the districts we visited.

Seeing time as an ally rather than an adversary may be critical to successful organizational communication. We live in a culture that wants instant results—but we also want to be consulted before any action is taken. Yosemite District Chancellor Tom Van Groningen has reflected on this contradiction and resolves it this way: "I've learned to be patient—and I'm equally persistent. If I think a proposal has merit, I'll pursue it. Keeping at it is the key. Over time this has contributed to stability and credibility."

The "No Surprises" Rule

In interviews with trustees, chancellors, presidents, deans, department heads, faculty leaders, and regular employees, the single most common observation related to communication was "no surprises." One person after another made it clear they did not want a decision, or the need to make a decision, sprung on them without warning. In the Yosemite district, the opportunity to purchase a piece of property with substantial facilities already in place came up unexpectedly. Understanding the "no surprises" rule, Chancellor Van Groningen immediately informed trustees by phone of the new opportunity. At a regular meeting of the District Council, he described the opportunity to his district and campus administrators and to the faculty leadership. The personnel director carried this information to the classified staff leadership. At the same time, Van Groningen sent a memo to all employees stating that the idea merited a feasibility study. In other words, before there was time for the information to leak through the organization and take the form of rumors about what the opportunity was and what commitments the district had made or might make, the information had been transmitted to all levels of leadership in the district and on the campuses. This chancellor had created a whole cadre of communicators in the organization *before* any decision choices were formulated, certainly before any decisions were made. Our interviews confirmed that key members of all groups within the organization were aware of this possible development. The message had penetrated.

We believe that effective communicating characterizes successful decision making. Sound governance encourages all members to communicate and requires communicative leaders.

Chapter Highlights

- Communication is a critical element of the process leading to a decision and of the process of implementing a decision.

- As messages get transmitted through many levels by means of many different individuals, much of the nuance and subtlety of the original communication will be lost.

- The negative, unintended effects of a badly conceived or badly executed communication can be significant, often undoing good work or requiring extensive time and energy to respond to those upset by the communication.

- A regular, predictable, well-understood communication structure is essential to creating a sense of trust and credibility among members of the organization. The wide variety of structures in the districts studied all shared these features: redundancy, multiple channels, clarity, and credibility. Each was made to function through effort, commitment, and a kind of institutionalized mutual respect that was reflected in the "no surprises" rule.

- All parties must believe that communication is open and honest, that all important information related to a decision has been made available, thus requiring that such information be provided *before* the decision is made. To ensure that information reaches all parts of the organization, repetitive and redundant communications must be employed.

- When a message is important enough that it must reach all parts of the organization, it should be presented in print (for example, by memo, in-house publications, posters, and signs), in speech (for example, at regular meetings, specially called meetings, informal contacts), and electronically (for example, voice mail, electronic mail, closed circuit television, telephone trees).

• Clarity is important both in the substance of a communication and in identifying the specific members of the organization to whom communications should be directed.

• Associated with clarity is credibility. Information must not only be understandable, but also must originate from a trustworthy source.

• Although "taking a lot of time" in communicating was often reported as a negative, organizations whose members give their time have real evidence of commitment on the part of their people.

• Seeing time as an ally rather than an adversary may be critical to successful organizational communication.

• In interviews with trustees, chancellors, presidents, deans, department heads, faculty leaders, and regular employees, the single most common observation related to communication was the "no surprises" rule.

Chapter Eight

Successful Governance:
What Really Matters

*"Life is the art of drawing sufficient conclusions
from insufficient premises."*
—Samuel Butler

Rather than conclude with a summary and recapitulation of what we have said in the first seven chapters, we wish to outline those themes and qualities that we believe are indicators of effective leadership in governance. These themes have emerged from our reflection on our research and reading, but are grounded in our experience and values. We emphasize the basis of our claims so readers can make an informed appraisal of our conclusions. Like Samuel Butler, we see this effort more as art than science.

We have arrived at these conclusions in two ways. First, we looked carefully at the material in the preceding chapters, identifying several key themes that provide the conceptual base of our work. Second, we returned to the interview data from our study institutions, filtering that material through our reading in the literature, our experience, and our own beliefs about what constitutes good practice, and arriving at a list of qualities that, for us, characterize the best institutional governance. The conceptual themes provide a more reflective and analytical approach to leadership and governance in the community college whereas the list of qualities reflects a more pragmatic orientation, providing a practical checklist for institutional self-assessment. Since we believe the conceptual and practical are interdependent, our discussion treats them that way.

Many practitioners, facing more tasks than can be completed in a day, look upon the conceptual and the philosophical as a luxury option, something to address when other issues are not pressing. Working on a dozen disparate assignments with time for half that many, the busy practitioner is immersed in the practical and concrete, looking for ways to simplify. Thinking into the meanings and values of what one does is difficult and time-consuming; many see such activity as an add-on, just one more assignment, and not one the boss seems to have much interest in, at that. In those circumstances, complexity, conceptual frameworks, and underlying value assumptions seem irrelevant to the crisis of the moment.

We have commented on the crucial difference between the urgent and the important. By adopting an exclusively pragmatic orientation, practitioners risk missing much of the rich and complex meaning that the practical realities of their work are built upon. Missing such meanings often damages the effectiveness of these practitioners both in dealing with the crisis of the moment and in leading the many people and the multiple constituencies they must work with.

Preoccupation with the practical, the here and now, seems particularly acute among community college administrators, partly, perhaps, because of the characteristics of the people who are attracted to administration, partly because of their work load, partly because the culture of the institution places high value on ready response, partly because a large portion of the educational program and the faculty focus on applied learning, and partly because the academic background and preparation of presidents tend to be more applied than theoretical. In his study of the community college presidency George Vaughan describes the academic preparation of presidents: "77 percent of the community college presidents with doctorates have their highest degree in education, and although almost 32 percent of them have Ph.D.'s, a large number of the Ph.D.'s are in education rather than in an academic discipline. . . . Since World War II the academic study of higher education has developed as an applied field of study and is becoming increasingly important for the preparation of middle-level administrators" (1986, p. 19).

Regardless of how practical the busy manager wishes to be, no one in an educational institution exhibits value-free behavior or behaves in ways that are not based on underlying conceptual and theoretical assumptions, conscious or unconscious. Our experience suggests that the leaders who have a firm sense of institutional mission and a clear view of how their organization works avoid much wasted motion. Busyness should never be equated with the business of the college. Practitioners can either develop a knowledge of the implicit values and conceptual foundations of their behavior or remain ignorant of them. Clearly, our work is addressed to those who seek deeper understanding of leadership in decision making and communication in the modern community college. We speak to the person Donald Schön (1983) calls "the reflective practitioner."

Conceptual Themes

The most important of our conceptual themes are these:

- Striving, aspiration, the sense in individuals and institutions that they are unfinished, that they can be improved, and that the effort is worthwhile
- Ambiguity, complexity, paradox—the working conditions of organizational practitioners
- The dominant role of history in organizations: the fact that the consequences of today's actions create conditions under which tomorrow's decisions are taken
- The controlling effect that leaders' beliefs about their followers have on the followers' beliefs about their leaders
- The role of personalities in institutions
- The enormous fund of power created by everyone's capacity to decide
- Governance as a context-specific, climate-controlling activity
- Leadership in governance

The Quest to Improve. A distinguished friend of ours on the faculty of a major research university once decried what he called the "myth of improvement," the wrongheaded sense that good institutions ought to be "improved." He believed that his university, for example, was working quite well, thank you very much, and the effort to improve it could easily damage something that was functioning effectively or replace it with something that did not work nearly as well. Indeed, "If it ain't broke, don't fix it" is often good advice. It ignores, however, important needs for preventive maintenance, which, if neglected, will lead to breakdowns. It also ignores the capacity for intellectual and spiritual growth in human beings. It ignores the capacity in institutions for acting more humanely, for achieving their mission more effectively.

Throughout our interviews and conversations with community college practitioners, we have encountered the search for excellence, a striving to improve. We did not find large reservoirs of self-satisfaction and complacency. At Miami-Dade we heard the quip, "If we're the best, God help the rest," a statement reflecting people's clear sense that the place was imperfect, that they could make an already outstanding college even better. In many ways our study institutions operated on tentatives rather than tenets. There was a readiness to change existing practices and structures when better ones could be found, and there was also a willingness to engage in the search. "Constant, purposeful innovation" is one of the mottos of De Anza College's founding president, Bob De Hart. "Excellence is a journey, not a destination," he says. Striving, therefore, is one theme of our work, the quest for better practice, more useful structures, deeper understanding. The best institutions convey a sense that the work, and the people who do it, are always still being created. The community colleges we studied reflect that belief. And everyone made it clear that they gave their time and energy and commitment because the journey was worth the effort.

Ambiguity, Paradox, Complexity. At the same time, in the same institutions, apparently contradictory ideas are found. For example, people show a sense of pride in what exists and what has been accomplished. They feel good about the institution and its service to students. What is working well does not need fixing. So, in the best institutions the culture reflects the ambiguity, paradox, and complexity of things. Albert Einstein once observed that everything should be made as simple as possible, but no simpler. In organizations, things are almost always more complicated than they seem. In this book we have identified and described institutions that are replete with imperfections but are working hard to achieve excellence. Many organizations, in our view, either do not aspire to their maximum potential or they adopt strategies that frustrate achieving this goal. Paradoxically, community colleges, with all their conceptual ambiguity and multiple roles, may possess qualities that permit the sustained pursuit of institutional excellence, while those higher education institutions best described as anarchical or political may not be capable of something that could reasonably be called an institutional aspiration. Concepts of family, teaching as preeminent purpose, institutional teamwork, and esprit may not apply in these institutions as they can in community colleges. When everyone is pursuing independent research interests as a way of life, an overarching institutional mission may be merely extra baggage.

Recent findings by The Carnegie Foundation for the Advancement of Teaching affirm our view. In its 1989 survey of the attitudes of the American professoriate, the foundation found "important differences" between two-year and four-year college and university faculty. The foundation says, "Community college teachers have the clearest sense of purpose of any sector of higher education and feel good about their institution" (1990, p. 24). Community college faculty "show a clear commitment to teaching as well as high expectations about the quality of that teaching. . . . We believe that this clarity of purpose—this lack of tension over values and expectations—helps explain the higher personal satisfaction displayed by community college faculty members. . . . Perhaps the most startling statistic is the response to the simple question, 'How do you feel about your institution?' Sixty-five percent of two-year faculty rated it 'a very good place for me.' Only 41 percent at four-year colleges could reply as positively" (p. 25).

We believe this difference of focus between institutions whose dominant mission is teaching versus those whose dominant mission is research, or whose mission is suspended between the two, shapes the governance process in character-defining ways. In Birnbaum's collegial institution, the institutional culture can value an aspiration to render more effective service to students. In the bureaucratic institution the rational effort to serve a diverse student population can be infused with the ambition to do it with maximum effectiveness. In organized anarchies and political institutions, where the research interests of the faculty vie for preeminence with the teaching mission, the forces that drive research and academic inquiry make establishing the student as the focus of institutional effort very difficult indeed.

Administrators who seek maximum success for their institutions must develop a sensitivity to the complexities of leadership. Birnbaum suggests that presidents should "complicate themselves" by learning to look at their institutions through multiple frames of reference (1988, p. 208). The structural, human resource, political, and symbolic perspectives that we discussed in Chapter Five are enormously useful for this purpose. Within the multiple realities of complex organizations, every person has legitimate needs and interests. Responding reasonably and fairly to these interests is a complicated task essential to our conception of leadership. Simple understandings lead to general rules that administrators mistakenly try to apply to all situations. Complex understandings suggest that different principles apply in different situations and that what succeeded in the past may fail in the present or future. Thus, in Birnbaum's words, "The only thing more useful than a good theory is a lot of good theories" (p. 209).

The Past as Creator of the Future. "I am a part of all that I have met," Tennyson's Ulysses says. In the same way, institutions are part of all they have experienced. Most of us understand that actions taken today shape tomorrow. We are less aware of how actions taken yesterday formed and shaped today. Today often seems quite new to us. Yet history is a powerful creator of both the present and the future. The working out of some "ancient grudge" between the Montagues and Capulets set the tragedy of Romeo and Juliet in motion. Cherished enmities and burnished grievances have the same effect for individuals and groups in institutions. Additionally, through the repetition of routines, history creates habits in institutions, habitual ways of doing things, habitual relationships among individuals and constituencies, and habitual orientations to problems or challenges. Such habits create distinctive competencies or inadequacies. Recognizing the historical basis for important strengths allows leaders to reinforce those organizational elements. Knowing that certain institutional weaknesses are grounded in the past is the first step in changing those conditions.

Both internal and external histories affect the affairs of institutions. Externally, in California the long history of excessive legislation relating to education has its roots in the fact that California law is based on old Spanish law. The Spanish system held that if the law does not expressly grant permission to do a thing, one is forbidden from doing it. English law, in contrast, holds that if the law does not prohibit one from doing a thing, one is permitted to do it. Thus in California, many of the over 2,000 statutes relating to community colleges simply grant the institutions permission to do some routine thing, such as maintaining student records. Even though the legislature a few years ago enacted a so-called permissive education code, ostensibly creating an English law model, the history of excessive legislation continues. In the 1989 legislative session, about 250 bills relating to California community colleges were introduced. Both legislators and their constituents in the colleges have not yet changed the habit of attempting to legislate everything.

Within colleges, habits created over time have a powerful effect on institutional competency. Boards of trustees, for example, develop habits of playing the executive's role, making effective governance impossible. Managements and unions develop habits of mistrust and hostility and, before long, these become the only patterns of interaction people are comfortable with. Leaders need to remember that today's behavior, today's relationships, and today's decisions both create tomorrow and are often recapitulated in it. It may be that the habits of history can reach a kind of critical mass, so that no amicable solution can ever be found. In many states there are institutions that have for decades been known as problem cases—fractious, contentious, quarrelsome, unhappy. People at every level who care for their institutions should go to great lengths to prevent such decay from setting in.

What Leaders Believe About Their Followers. The governed have always held a healthy skepticism toward those governing them, a notion reflected in our epigraph to Chapter One. This age, however, seems to have transformed skepticism into cynicism, profound mistrust, almost hostility toward leaders. The posthumous exposés of Presidents John Kennedy and Lyndon Johnson, the Watergate affair and President Richard Nixon's self-discrediting declaration, "I am not a crook," have confirmed the worst suspicions of many that leaders are not to be believed, nor even, in many cases, to be followed. The political transformations in Central and Eastern Europe begun in 1989 reflect a similar relationship between leaders and followers. What followers think of their leaders is enormously important, for no one can lead if no one will follow.

What leaders think of their followers is equally important. In Dostoevsky's *The Brothers Karamazov* the Grand Inquisitor believed that people would go to any lengths to escape the responsibilities of freedom; thus, it was the duty of the medieval church to control its brutish, selfish, infantile petitioners through the exercise of miracle, mystery, and authority. Rousseau offered a contrary view of human nature. He believed that man is born majestic and free, but is everywhere in chains, bound by oppressive institutions rather than anything inherent in himself. We know that, at their worst, human beings are fully capable of validating the Grand Inquisitor's darkest beliefs; at their best, they confirm Rousseau's optimism. Which extreme people move toward is evoked in part by the behavior of those in organizational authority.

After years of both studying and modeling leadership, John Gardner concludes: "The conventional question is, 'Do the followers believe in the leaders?' A more searching question is, 'Does the leader believe in the followers?' " (1986, p. 6). Gardner sees great unused gifts among our nation's people, gifts that could be tapped to help meet the enormous needs for leadership in our complex society. But, he says, "You have to have faith in human possibilities. Your chance of awakening the possibilities in others depends heavily upon you yourself having faith in them" (p. 6).

We believe there are immense unused gifts among the people in our institutions. Ordinary people are capable of extraordinary contributions, given the right conditions. Leaders' beliefs concerning their followers, whether positive or negative, become self-fulfilling prophecies. When leaders express a fundamental belief in the capacity of human beings to serve greatly, a belief and reliance on the best that is in people, an institution can achieve its maximum potential. Such a belief was set forth in a conference presentation by Mary Wallace Wheat, a trustee in the Foothill-De Anza district: "At one point in my evolution as a trustee, I believed that only trustees could make major decisions because only they could see the big picture. I no longer believe that. Given the opportunity, the information, the commitment to the institution, and, most particularly, to the students it serves, people of good will throughout an institution can gather together and make wise, thoughtful, constructive, far-reaching decisions for the benefit of the whole, not for individual personal gain."

The Role of Personalities. The role personalities play in the affairs of institutions varies among and within organization types. No one would dispute that an enormously important role has been played by the personalities of William Hewlett and David Packard in the Hewlett-Packard Company. Similarly, Max De Pree and his father before him have played the dominant role in shaping the Herman Miller Furniture Company. In higher education things seem a bit more complicated. To the extent that certain institutions are accurately described as organized anarchies, personalities may count for less. When no one is in charge, what difference do the personalities of those not in charge make? On the other hand, when the organization chart does in fact say something about the way decisions are made, when authority is exercised by someone, the personality of the individual exercising it takes on more significance.

Individual values are a key factor in understanding the role of personalities in organizations. For example, administrators who are impatient with processes for involving people in decisions, who want "to get on with it," or "to get the job done," are reflecting a set of values. These values imply that ends are important, means, perhaps not. They imply, in fact, that people are only means, not ends, in the organization. If people are ends as well as means, they must be respected; their views must be sought out and taken into account; one cannot surprise or manipulate them. The degree to which people are valued in the organization controls, to a large extent, the quality of work life for participants in the organization. In this area—the quality of work life—the principal effect of personalities is felt. We believe leaders can listen carefully to people, be sensitive to issues of process in the institution, and still exhibit the "bias for action" that Peters and Waterman (1982) found characteristic of the excellent companies. Some years ago when Foothill-De Anza's newly formed Budget and Policy Development Group (BPDG) was struggling to find a less ponderous and time-consuming style of operation, an administrator in the group stated that if all the district's innovative programs had needed BPDG approval, many would not exist today. A faculty leader in the group disagreed, saying, "Not only would they have been created, but if the questions asked in the BPDG had been asked beforehand and more people had bought in up front, those programs would suffer from fewer problems today." We agree with the faculty member. Institutions must embrace the paradox of being at once biased toward action and biased toward broad participation and partnership in governance.

The way particular individuals engage one another in the organization facilitates or impedes participation. Yet, just as the role of the personalities of leaders at every level should not be denied, neither should it be overemphasized. Our sense of the role of individuals in community college organizations is roughly this: by the values they reflect in their behavior, authority figures affect the quality of work life for people in the institution; this quality of life has a significant effect on people's morale; morale affects the commitment people are willing to make to the enterprise beyond mere compliance with the minimums expected of them; a high degree of such commitment characterizes great institutions.

Reservoirs of Power. In organizations, decision makers possess power. Everyone in every organization is a decision maker. This means that everyone owns power. Persons who prepare and administer budgets are familiar with the term *cost center.* A cost center is an identified unit in the administrative structure where budgeted revenues and expenditures are aggregated and accounted for. We suggest an analogous term in thinking about institutional governance: *power center.* Every person in the organization is a power center. The reservoir created by the aggregation of power from the individual centers is immense.

The management of any organization has limited control over these individual power centers and that control is limited to achieving compliance, or the appearance of compliance, with job requirements, policies, rules, and regulations. When everyone simply does the job, complying with what is expected, the results are adequacy—an institution judged satisfactory, yet quite unexceptional. Some individuals will never do more than simply comply. Some few will not even do that. Yet another small group will give a great deal more than the minimum no matter what the level of organizational neglect, abuse, or impediment. We contend, however, that every organization possesses a number of people who are capable of contributing a great deal more to the enterprise than simple compliance. Those people are particularly affected by the organization's climate, the ambient conditions from which members derive a sense of efficacy, a feeling of being valued, a belief they are respected. When the climate is deficient, these people will not function as well. When the climate is positive and supportive, these same people will respond with high-level efforts.

Our experience and observations in our study institutions suggest that the community college mission rests on values that are important to community college people: access, diversity, community, responsiveness, attention to every student, cultural pluralism. These values should be clearly articulated and embodied in the behavior of administrators and other organizational leaders. The more power people can exercise as partners in governance, the more they will use both the power granted them and the power they already possess in the service of the institution's mission. Since power is inherent in decision making, and decision making is at the heart of institutional governance, governance is a climate-controlling activity.

Governance as a Climate-Controlling Activity. Workers at every level respond to cues from the environment. From these cues they gain impressions of whether they are valued and respected by the organization, whether they can be proud of their work. The most important of these cues come from people above them in the structure. These impressions are translated, often unconsciously, into feelings, either positive or negative, and such feelings are the principal component of a worker's morale. Morale, the way one feels about one's work, is a key factor in determining the commitment many employees are willing to make to their work.

Quite a large number of factors contribute to creating a worker's morale. First among them, we believe, is the individual's own personality: a highly stable configuration of elements that are not easily, if at all, changed in spite of either positive or negative conditions in the workplace. Barry Staw's (1986) research at the University of California, Berkeley, seems to confirm that adult workers come into their jobs predisposed to be happy and productive or unhappy and unproductive. These basic tendencies, however, are not impervious to conditions in the workplace, and other factors influence workers' morale as well. One's level of compensation plays a role in creating morale. So does the physical environment of the workplace and the tools one is given to do one's job. The personalities and social characteristics of one's boss and one's fellow workers are important. Beyond these considerations, we believe that the way the workplace is governed is crucial in creating the way people feel about their work.

People feel a sense of ownership and responsibility when they make decisions and when they take part in the decision-making process. On the other hand, if people routinely hear about decisions only after they are made, if decisions they have participated in are routinely changed by some authority figure, if people are often surprised by decisions, if people feel ignored or, worse, manipulated, those people will hardly feel good about their workplace. Such conditions contribute to a compliance-only orientation on the part of workers.

Conversely, if people legitimately participate in processes of deciding—and for us "legitimate" means having a say, being heard, and being represented when the real decisions are made—their feelings of responsibility are increased, their sense that they are valued by the organization is enlarged, and their commitment to institutional purposes is enhanced. Thus, governance processes, as much as any other single factor, affect the climate of the institution.

Leadership in Governance. We have defined leadership in governance as the creation of conditions, through institutional processes for decision making and communication, which commit organizational participants to the service of institutional purposes, acting beyond mere compliance with the mandates of their jobs. People take on the spirit of the institution; they internalize its values. Such commitment affects the quality of their work, the care and attention they give to students and co-workers, and the extent of the contribution they are willing to make. Other definitions of leadership can apply to community college administration, but we believe that fully involving people in governance will aid an institution in achieving its maximum potential.

Leadership in governance includes these five elements. First, persons who wish to be leaders need to embody or articulate in visible and authentic ways a goal, an ideal, that captures the highest values and finest purposes of the institution. Such goals strike deep chords in people, provide inspiration and direction, and are ideals to be pursued, but never fully achieved. Such purposes should be set forth at every level, for every administrative unit in the institution. Presidents and chancellors should articulate such purposes. So should deans, vice presidents, directors, and department heads as well as union leaders, senate leaders, and leaders of other governance entities. Second, with such goals serving as compass needles setting direction, those who wish to lead should seek ways to empower people, conferring upon them the authority to make things happen that serve institutional goals. Governance is one of the most useful instruments for conveying power to people. Third, standards of excellence, articulated as part of the essential vision, must be sustained. People must be held accountable. No one—in any part of the organization—has the right to abuse his or her power, whether that power derives from the authority of office or from the power granted to organizational members. Fourth, we insist on the paradox that even though power has been "given away," the responsibility of office has not been signed over to others and thereby abdicated. We are not talking about officials who avoid taking a position because some group took a vote on an issue. Officials must retain their responsibility, they must make decisions, and they must be held to account for them. Fifth, we envision a partnership in decision making in which three things occur: (1) responsibility and accountability are retained by organizational officials; (2) these officials find means to incorporate the legitimate views and interests of everyone in their decisions—people feel they have had their say, that it was heard, and that it was thoughtfully considered even if it was not agreed to; and (3) people are provided the means to achieve—they can decide, act, and react in the service of institutional purposes.

No single, uniform structure can be installed everywhere to accomplish this. Rather, we are convinced that different structures and different strategies will emerge in different places in response to particular institutional conditions. We think the Peters and Waterman notion of "simultaneous loose-tight properties" (1982, p. 318) points the way. This idea suggests that we should be very clear, very tight—even rigid—on values, but very loose, granting wide latitude and autonomy, on the means for achieving goals based on those values.

Qualities of the Best Governance Practice

Though the colleges we studied varied in size, geography, demographics, and structure, we found qualities common to every institution. The most effective governance in community colleges includes the widely shared perception that decision-making and communication processes possess three characteristics: *clarity, openness,* and *fairness.* This perception develops most fully in the college in the presence of two key attributes: *competence* and *stability.* All of these qualities both create and are created by *trust* which is always characteristic of the best in governance practice; and finally the entire apparatus for governance operates under institutional conditions of widely shared *personal commitment, civility, caring, hard work,* and *good times.* These eleven terms, then, constitute the central core of our sense of the best institutional governance: clarity, openness, fairness, competence, stability, trust, commitment, civility, caring, hard work, and good times. Briefly, here is what we mean by each of them.

Clarity refers to widely shared knowledge among organizational participants of what decision-making structures and processes are. There is little confusion on how things work, and everyone shares essentially the same working understandings. The president, for example, does not describe the time, place, and manner of decision making in one way while his or her administrative staff or faculty describe it in another way. Everyone knows the governance mechanisms and there is general congruity among the college's constituencies that these mechanisms work in commonly understood ways.

People can be very clear on the way governance works in their institution and at the same time feel that it is characterized by secrets and deceit. *Openness* means a perception on the part of organizational participants both that they have access to decision-making processes and that the information available to them for use in these processes constitutes the truth, the whole truth, and nothing but the truth. Openness requires honesty in information, full and timely disclosure, an absence of manipulation, and access, either in person or through representation, to the arenas in which decisions are made. Not everyone, of course, wishes to participate in institutional governance. But people feel that governance processes are open to them and that they can get into the act when they want to.

A shared sense that *fairness* characterizes decision making means that people at every level in the organization and in every classification feel their needs and views are being heard, listened to, and taken into account. People feel that nonsqueaky wheels get grease, too, and that processes are not dominated by those who choose to show up and speak. It also means that the organization's resources and rewards are distributed in such a way that favorites do not get more and that everyone feels she receives an equitable share or at least an equal opportunity to plead her case and be fairly considered. The management of Birnbaum's ideal institution is sensitive to "negative feedback loops" (1988, p. 179) in which problems are quickly sensed and addressed. We agree with the importance of such negative feedback loops, but we go further. The most effective institutions attempt to anticipate the potential for negative feedback before it occurs and change the conditions that give rise to it.

We have stated that we believe that personalities play a significant role in the affairs of institutions, but we have also concluded something else: while excellence can be achieved in organizations led by persons who are enormously dissimilar, all these people share at least one characteristic in common, a high degree of *competence*. Excellent leaders can be tall or short, physically attractive or unattractive, quiet or garrulous, urbane or folksy, but they are all fundamentally competent, proficient in the work they do. We believe that an institution cannot achieve its maximum potential, for example, with an incompetent board of trustees or chief executive officer or with incompetents serving in any of its key leadership roles, in the faculty, the administration, or in the support staff. Among the desirable characteristics of leaders identified by Kouzes and Posner (1987), competence ranks second only to honesty.

We also believe that *stability* is essential. Often faculty, administrators, and staff of long tenure in institutions see persons at the top come and go. When rank and file people conclude that their leaders are merely passing through, presumably on their way to bigger and better things, they lose faith that these "leaders" have the institution's best interests at heart. If there is confusion created by frequent turnover at the top, either in the governing board or the top ranks of administration, the underpinnings that excellence must be built upon fail. In describing high-performing systems Vaill (1982, p. 23) affirms the necessity of stability: "It is of great importance that . . . leaders put in large amounts of both microtime and macrotime. Microtime is the hour-to-hour, day-to-day kind of investment. Less frequently noted is macrotime—that is, leaders of high-performing systems tend to stay in their jobs for many years; they do not simply 'pass through.' "

A widely shared sense of mutual *trust* is essential for excellence in governance. All the parties must feel that the others are telling the truth, the whole truth, and nothing but the truth, that they are not manipulative or motivated by hidden agendas and can be depended upon to keep their word—that the parties are, in a word, honest. Trust can exist only where people are trustworthy. Trust also requires that each of the parties respect the legitimate standing of the others and acknowledge that everyone possesses rights deriving from being a stakeholder in the enterprise. Trustees and CEOs are as susceptible as anyone else to serving narrow personal interests. When these officials use their positions to further those interests, a great deal is at risk in the institution. So much begins at the top in organizations, a truth that led us to the paradox that organizations turn the structure of buildings upside down. In buildings the foundation is at the bottom; in organizations it is also at the top. Policies are created at the top, environments are formed, values are reinforced, and resources are allocated. We believe that the basic foundation for trust is also created at the top. On the question of whose responsibility it is to trust first, Kouzes and Posner say, "Trust is a risk game. The leader must ante up first. If leaders want to be seen as trustworthy, they must first give evidence of their own trust in us" (1987, p. 19).

Our belief is that the best institutions are characterized by large numbers of people who exhibit a high degree of *personal commitment* to the mission of the enterprise. Such persons understand the institution's mission, accept and value it, have at least a latent understanding of the organization as a means to achieve the mission, and do not draw hard lines around the minimum requirements of their job—they want to do more than the minimum. Inspiring people with a sense of the institution's possibilities and granting people power to do their part in realizing those possibilities creates in them commitment to the enterprise and they will share responsibility for its failures as well as its successes.

In some organizations common courtesy—*civility*—is not so common. Interaction among the parties in such places includes name calling and mean-spirited personal attacks. People openly display a lack of respect for one another. They seem not to like each other. In some of the worst situations loud, angry, public (and private) arguments take place aimed at individuals rather than issues. Such conditions, without exception, drain the organization of the intellectual and emotional energy necessary to achieve maximum and, in some cases, even minimum effectiveness. "Sticks and stones can break your bones, but words cause permanent damage." This wisecrack by Barry Champlain, the "shock jock" in the 1988 film *Talk Radio*, conveys a meaning that is important. Words cause wounds that may heal, but scar tissue remains forever. In the best institutions, cultural norms reinforce courtesy and civility as dominant qualities in interpersonal relations.

Caring is a feeling. It is related to commitment and civility both as a cause and an effect. The dominant characteristics of commitment are intellectual. The dominant qualities of caring are emotional, but the emotions and the intellect are intertwined in both. In our study we found large numbers of individuals who were deeply interested in their institutions, who were concerned with their functioning and well-being, who profoundly cared about their colleges and their colleagues.

Such caring is an essential prerequisite to another of the conditions we believe to be characteristic of the best in governance practice: *hard work*. Hard work everywhere, at every level, by many people. We have seen the enormous amounts of time and energy freely given by many individuals in the best institutions. Once, in a discussion in Foothill-De Anza of how much time was consumed in the hard work of the Budget and Policy Development Group, one of the members reminded the assembly of Mae West's marvelous line: "Anything worth doing is worth doing slowly." Such caring and commitment reflect a sense of pride and joy in people, a "he ain't heavy, he's my brother" willingness to make processes for decision making and communication effectively serve the purposes of the institution.

Which brings us to the last of the qualities we identify in the best governance processes: the people involved are having a *good time*. A sense of playfulness and camaraderie arises in large part out of the other ten qualities; a good humor pervades events and relationships. People don't take themselves too seriously. There is a lot of good-natured kidding around. Participants have fun, seeing the lighter side, even when matters are of great import and seriousness. Such a quality among the players creates the clear perception that their role in the institutional drama is a joy to play.

What creates these conditions in an institution? We have not found the complete answer to that question. Our work identifies some important factors, but there is much to be learned about the complex interplay of leadership and governance. All eleven of the qualities, we emphasize, are not fully developed in any of the colleges we looked at. But many institutions have a richer mix of these qualities than others. We believe the influence that makes the greatest difference in achieving their fullest realization is leadership in governance.

Resource A:

Institutional Profiles

Note: All enrollment figures taken from AACJC Membership Directory, 1990.

Allan Hancock College

Location: Santa Maria, California
Founded: 1920 (as Santa Maria Junior College)
Credit Enrollment: 8,510
Board of Trustees: 5 members, elected at large, each represent-
ing a specific trustee area, for 4-year terms. Trustees must be
residents and qualified voters in trustee area they represent.
President: Gary R. Edelbrock
Organization: Single campus; CEO title: Superintendent-
President
Faculty: 125
Administrators: 25
Classified Staff: 168
Annual Budget: $25,683,000
Collective Bargaining: Faculty—no bargaining agent; Classi-
fied—California School Employees Association, Chapter #251
Philosophy:

> The philosophy of Allan Hancock College re-
> flects the conviction that education is a lifelong
> quest. The college exists as a center of learning
> which guarantees access to all who can benefit. It
> offers each individual the opportunity to identify
> and realize educational objectives in pursuit of a
> full and productive life. The college fosters the
> development of human potential through a com-
> prehensive program of courses and services which
> promote educational, social, and cultural enrich-
> ment in an environment of inquiry and civility.
> Allan Hancock College believes in a close rela-
> tionship between students and faculty, college
> and community. Its dedication to academic free-
> dom encourages an open exchange and explo-
> ration of ideas. The college is committed to
> excellence in learning, in teaching, and in service
> [*Catalogue*, p. 5].

District Governance Structure (key decision-making groups):
- Board of Trustees (meets monthly; special meetings as needed).
- President's Cabinet (president and 4 vice presidents) (meets weekly).
- President's Council (all managers) (meets monthly).
- Academic Senate: 30 senators, 1 per 5 faculty; Executive Committee (3 officers, 2 at-large senators, all serving two-year terms); Personnel; Budget and Finance; Academic Policy and Planning; Student Affairs and Services; Elections; Administrator Review; Staff Development; Vocational Education. Established in 1968, the Academic Policy and Planning Committee consists of members elected from each department, one from counseling, and one student representative. The chair is elected by the members for a two-year term. The vice president, Instruction, is an ex-officio member, without vote. The committee considers all curriculum proposals, academic standards, and coordination of instructional planning and practices (meets weekly).
- Department Chairs—most are elected by faculty (meets weekly).
- Deans and Directors Forum (both Academic Affairs and Student Services—primarily for coordination and communication) (meets monthly).
- Faculty Association (affiliated with California Teachers Association): the Association's Salary Committee compares the faculty salary schedule, fringe benefits, and hourly instructional rates of the college to those of the 24 California community college districts whose relative revenue (income per ADA) are the closest to Allan Hancock College's. After informal communications between the faculty association and the administration, an annual salary report is formally presented to the board of trustees each spring.
- Associate Faculty: representing part-time faculty, independently communicates with the administration and board of trustees (meets twice a semester with president).

- California School Employees Association—bargaining agent for all classified employees, excluding managers, supervisors, and confidentials.

Budget Decision Process: Currently, a comprehensive planning model drawing together educational and facilities masterplans and budget development is being formulated by a comprehensive planning committee representing faculty, administrators, and classified employees. Once completed, this framework will be used for budget review. In the interim, the traditional budget process is followed: Departments review previous year's budgets and suggest changes. These proposals are reviewed by a budget analyst, the appropriate associate superintendent, the vice president, and the manager of the area. The budget analyst works with guidelines to control specified budget categories. Draft budget is assembled in Administrative Services. Income estimates are developed by vice president, Administrative Services, and president. Conflicts and competitions for budget allocations are resolved in president's cabinet and, ultimately, by superintendent-president. Formal budget adopted by board of trustees in early September. Board receives quarterly status reports and a mid-year budget adjustment takes place in January.

Policy Change Decision Process (establishing a new academic calendar): Proposal to consider adopting "early" semester calendar is developed and presented to academic senate executive committee. College president appears before full senate to make presentation and answer questions. Student poll is conducted; students favor change. Faculty votes approval by narrow margin. Based on both discussion and support, administration consolidates proposal and takes it to board of trustees for approval. (One faculty member commented: "I lost on the calendar issue, but we had a full discussion among the faculty before the decision. I was heard.")

Foothill-De Anza Community College District

Location: Los Altos Hills, California
Founded: 1957

Credit Enrollment: 47,465
Board of Trustees: 5 members, elected to 4-year terms in odd-numbered years, plus 1 nonvoting student
Chancellor: Thomas W. Fryer, Jr.
Organization: Multicollege (separate accreditation for each college); district CEO title—Chancellor and District Superintendent
Colleges: 2 colleges, each headed by a president: De Anza, Foothill
Faculty: 520 full-time
Administrators: 74
Classified Staff: 560
Annual Budget: $110 million
Collective Bargaining: Foothill-De Anza Faculty Association—unaffiliated; California School Employees, Chapter 96 (maintenance and skilled trades) and Chapter 4316 (clerical-technical)
Philosophy:

The Mission: This statement is based upon the premise that the philosophy, mission, and priorities of the Foothill-De Anza Community College District are properly established by The Board of Trustees of the District.

The Foothill-De Anza Community College District, responding to community needs, exists to provide high quality educational opportunities that promote development of individual abilities and enhance the quality of community life.

The Board of Trustees pursues this mission through the programs and services of two comprehensive community colleges supported by a central services organization.

The Mission rests on these assumed values:

1. Foothill-De Anza Community College District is an organization of people for people, whose purpose is to serve students by

- transmitting knowledge
- developing human potential and creativity
- cultivating responsible citizenship
- promoting excellence in individuals and groups
- supplying educational resources, both faculties and facilities
- recognizing the ethnic diversity of its communities and student groups
- fostering intercultural and international understanding.

2. Foothill-De Anza must provide quality educational opportunities which are equitable, effective, efficient, and convenient.
3. Recognizing all people possess dignity as individuals, Foothill-De Anza will not compromise the dignity of anyone.
4. Every individual representing Foothill-De Anza is to contribute to fulfilling the District's stated mission and to act at all times in ways that reflect positively upon the district.
5. Students are here to learn and contribute actively to the educational process.
6. The unique identities of the Colleges contribute to fulfilling the District's mission.
7. Foothill-De Anza must be operated on a fiscally sound basis without compromising its basic mission ["The Philosophy, Mission, and Priorities of the Foothill-De Anza Community College District," 1990].

District Governance Structure (key decision-making groups):
- Board of Trustees (meets twice monthly).
- Chancellor's Cabinet (Budget and Policy Develop-

ment Group): chancellor, 2 college presidents, general counsel, directors of Business Services, Operations, and Human Resources, presidents of faculty senates, faculty association, both chapters of California School Employees Association, both associated student bodies, and the administrative management association, chief negotiators for three unions, two academic division deans, and a representative of the Minority Staff Association (meets twice monthly).

- Faculty Association: 17-member executive board, elected proportionately from each college; 4 seats set aside for part-time faculty; executive board elects association officers (meets weekly).

- District Faculty Senate: Constituted from leadership of the two college senates (meets monthly).

- California School Employees Association, Chapter 96—Skilled Trades and Crafts.

- California School Employees Association, Chapter 416—All other classified staff, except managers and confidential employees.

Budget Decision Process: Expenditure budget: in December, each college and Central Services develop requests from departments, working from preceding year's budget. Requests are consolidated and prioritized at each college and Central Services through reviews that include representatives of all employee groups. By February, these three budget proposals are assembled in district Business Services and sent to Budget and Policy Development Group (BPDG) for review and discussion. Faculty association budget analyst conducts concurrent study, working with director of Business Services. BPDG reviews and revises the allocation formula for distributing income among the two colleges and Central Services. The draft budget includes an initial set-aside for salary increases. Rough budget to board of trustees for information in April. Director, Business Services provides ongoing analysis of projected income to BPDG, which considers ways of both limiting expenditures and increasing income. Tentative budget goes to board in June; board adopts final budget in late July or early August.

Jefferson Community College

Location: Louisville, Kentucky
Founded: 1968
Credit Enrollment: 9,039
Board of Trustees: 7-member advisory board, appointed by governor; 4-year terms. "Local advisory boards . . . counsel with the respective community college administrators. This organizational structure, which preserved the organic relationship to the University and which allows autonomy and freedom to relate community college programs to the local communities, is distinctive and significant" (*Catalogue,* 1989–90, p. 12).
President: Ronald Horvath
Organization: Part of the University of Kentucky system; single college, multicampus, one accreditation process; the Community College System is headed by a chancellor who is directly responsible to the president of the University of Kentucky. The local community college president is responsible for general administration of each college.
Campuses: 2—each headed by a dean of Academic Affairs
Faculty: 225
Administrators: 30
Classified Staff: 120
Annual Budget: $13,779,728
Collective Bargaining: None
Philosophy and Values:

> Jefferson Community College's philosophy and values have been refined and published as part of a campus-wide project to state to the public and the student body what the institution represents. The complete statement which resulted from this "Institutional Values Project" can be obtained from the President's Office. . . .
>
> Our primary goal is to be an institution of high quality, operated by dedicated people providing educational services and opportunities

which meet the needs of our students and community. We aspire to be recognized in our community as a caring institution, dedicated to high academic standards in our credit and non-credit programs. As a publicly supported community college, we make every effort to provide opportunities for the educational development of our students and a fulfilling work environment for our faculty and staff. When students enroll in the College and when employees are hired, we expect them to commit themselves to these institutional values.

• We believe that the College staff holds the institution in trust for the citizens of Kentucky.

• We believe that the College exists to enable students to earn a college education.

• We believe that all College personnel must contribute to and be supportive of the educational mission of the College [*Catalogue*, 1989-90, p. 8].

District (College) Governance Structure (key decision-making groups):

• Advisory Board (meets once a month).

• "8 Group" (president, deans, budget director) (meets weekly).

• Faculty Council (division representatives: 5 Downtown; 4 Southwest; 2 nondivisional; and elected vice-chairs and secretaries for each campus; chaired by college president) (meets monthly).

• Faculty standing committees: Faculty Affairs Committee, Program Development Committee, Rules Committee.

• Administrative Committees: 30 in 1989-90 (e.g., Advisory Committee on Promotion and Tenure, Black Affairs Advisory Committee, Faculty Appeals Committee, Safety Committee, Writing Across the Curriculum).

Curriculum Decision Process (new course): Faculty member or program coordinator proposes to division chair; division approves and sends to program development committee of faculty council. After faculty council approval, course is voted on at faculty meeting. President consents and course is sent on to system level, where the system program development committee reviews and the system faculty council approves. Final approval comes from the University of Kentucky Chancellor of the Community College System.

Budget Decision Process: Expense budget begins at division level: annual budget proposal is prepared as part of the state-mandated five-year plans. The division proposals go to the president who works with academic deans in setting priorities. This version goes to a staff meeting as information and to a faculty council meeting as information. The expense budget is finally assembled by the president working with the business officer and it is sent to the UK Community College System chancellor for approval (where some priority changes may occur). On the income side, the state legislature (biennial) approves a University of Kentucky budget with a separate line item for the community college system. This budget faces line-item veto or reduction by the governor. Once adopted by legislature and governor, the UK president works with the UK chancellor, the medical center chancellor, and the community college chancellor in determining funding priorities. On this basis, the community college system chancellor will convey (when necessary) to Jefferson College the level of cuts (e.g., 1% or 3%) or the funding priorities needed in the proposed budget. The Jefferson president uses the "8 Group" to determine where to cut. These decisions go to staff meeting and division chairs as information.

Miami-Dade Community College

Location: Dade County, Florida
Founded: 1960
Credit Enrollment: 49,145
Board of Trustees: 7 members (5 until 1986); appointed by the governor; 4-year terms. "The Miami-Dade Community Col-

lege District Board of Trustees has responsibility and authority for proper operation of the College in accord with rules of
the State Board of Education and the State Board of Community Colleges. With recommendations and assistance from the
President of the College, the Board determines College policies, adopts regulations, prescribes standards, and exercises
other responsibilities assigned by law or necessary for improve-
ment of the College" (*Faculty Handbook and Service Directory*,
1988).
President: Robert H. McCabe
Organization: Multicampus (i.e., single institution-wide ac-
creditation); title of college CEO: president; title of campus
CEO: vice president.
Campuses: 5—each headed by a vice president: North, South,
Wolfson, Medical Center, Homestead
Faculty: 839
Administrators: 102
Nonfaculty Professionals: 180
Classified Staff: 1,231
Annual Budget: $139,247,727 (1989-90)
Collective Bargaining: None
Philosophy:

> To meet the higher educational needs of the com-
> munity, the faculty and the staff of Miami-Dade
> Community College are committed to the follow-
> ing concepts:
> • An intelligent and well-informed cit-
> izenry is necessary to the continuation and im-
> provement of the democratic way of life.
> • Individuals must be provided with the
> opportunity to develop their abilities to the ful-
> lest extent, consistent with their goals and with
> the expectations of society.
> • Individuals, through the educational
> process, may improve their capacities for partici-
> pating effectively in the processes of society and
> for sharing more abundantly in its culture.

• The College can significantly contribute to overcoming geographical, financial, and admission barriers which inhibit opportunities for higher education.

• The programs and services of the College should be of the highest quality possible.

• The fostering of freedom of inquiry is a fundamental responsibility of the faculty [*Faculty Handbook and Service Directory*, 1988, p. 3].

District (College) Governance Structure (key decision-making groups):

• Board of Trustees (meets once a month).

• Executive Committee (president and 8 vice presidents (meets once a month).

• President's Council (executive committee, faculty senate presidents (4), and faculty consortium president) (meets once a month).

• Budget Advisory Group (4 faculty, 4 district administrators, 5 campus administrators, 4 classified staff, consortium president, and chair of compensation committee).

• Compensation Committee (4 faculty and 4 support staff representatives, 2 district administrators, 1 campus administrator; makes recommendations on salary and benefits).

• Collegewide standing committees: Academic Affairs (4 deans, 4 faculty, and vice president, Education); Student Services (4 deans, 4 faculty, and vice president, Education); Administrative Services (4 deans, 4 faculty, and vice president, Administration).

• Faculty Senate Consortium (campus faculty senate presidents, at least one faculty representative per campus, and one additional representative for each additional 200 on that campus—currently 10 members). "This group functions not as a 'super senate,' but as trustee of the faculty members" (*Faculty Handbook . . .*, p. 8).

• Policy I-80, adopted as policy by the Board in 1977, established a separate faculty senate at each of the campuses, recognized by the administration as the official voice of the faculty on that campus. Each senate became a full partner with the campus administration in development and initiation of all matters related to educational and campus governance policies and procedures. Thereafter, all appointments of faculty to campus committees have been reviewed by senate presidents and appointments made with their concurrence (*Faculty Handbook* . . . , 1988, p. 8).

• Support Staff Council (campus-based): vehicle for support staff to bring concerns to campus vice president.

• Special projects outside of regular organizational structure:

1) Enrollment management project
2) Teaching-Learning Project
3) New Directions Project

Curriculum Decision Process (new course): Faculty member proposes course to department chair who takes it to associate dean who gets campus academic council approval. Academic dean takes it to college academic affairs committee. If proposal affects required core courses, college president must approve.

Budget Decision Process: College president establishes framework; budget advisory committee develops concept, using current budget, cost to continue based on enrollment forecast, applying staffing and growth formulas, student fee income from growth and state money for growth (more detailed decision process on campus); compensation committee recommends salary and benefits to president; final budget summary presented to board of trustees for review and approval.

Monroe Community College

Location: Rochester, New York
Founded: 1961
Credit Enrollment: 13,203
Board of Trustees: 10 voting members: 5 appointed by the Monroe County legislature and 4 by the governor of the state, for 9-year terms. A voting student board member is elected to a one-year term by the student body.

President: Peter A. Spina
Faculty: 304
Administrators: 56
Classified Staff: 306 civil service positions
Annual Budget: $52 million
Collective Bargaining: Faculty Association (affiliated with New York State Teachers and American Federation of Teachers); Civil Service Employees Association (contract negotiated by Monroe County); Stationary Engineers, Local 71-71A, International Union of Operating Engineers
Philosophy:

> Monroe Community College serves the educational needs of our community by providing learning opportunities for all who can benefit from instruction at a postsecondary level. By offering programs equivalent to the first two years of baccalaureate study, career-oriented programs leading to associate degrees, certificates, and programs in community services, we are dedicated to creating a comprehensive, learning-centered environment. Through careful planning and a realistic assessment of our resources, we strive to be both innovative and flexible in responding to the educational needs of the community.
>
> In serving students with a variety of interests and abilities, Monroe Community College places a high value on excellence in teaching as well as effective student services. The College encourages a respect for traditional verities and mastery of basic skills in its general education requirements. By sponsoring co-curricular events and by promoting community service programs of an educational and informative nature, the campus is a significant resource for enriching the community.
>
> In accomplishing its purpose, Monroe Community College enjoys strong support as a

vital part of the Rochester educational community, as an integral unit of the State University of New York, and as a purposeful institution of higher education dedicated to maintaining a national reputation for outstanding academic, educational, and administrative services [*Fact Book 1989*, p. 3].

District Governance Structure (key decision-making groups):
- Board of Trustees (committee structure: Finance and Facilities, Planning and Policies, Personnel and Programs, Nominating) (meets nine times per year).
- Executive Cabinet (president, vice presidents, executive assistant to president).
- Faculty Senate (which replaced Academic Governance Board in 1989) (departments elect one to three representatives based on size); Executive Committee (officers and chairs of standing committees); Standing Committees: Academic Policies; Curriculum; Planning; Professional Development; Special Committee on Administrative Affairs; Nominations, Elections, and Governance.
- Faculty Association (executive committee and seven standing committees); bargaining agent since 1967.
- Monroe Community College Association, Inc.: funded by student fees and revenues from bookstore and other programs; operates a range of services including bookstore, food service, child care and health care; managed by board of directors (4 students, 2 faculty, 3 administration, 1 staff, 1 alumnus).

Budget Decision Process: Strategic Planning Committee establishes guidelines; president develops revenue estimates in October (current income sources: 38% from state, 18% from county, 31% from student fees, 13% from other sources) and consults with union and senate presidents; divisions get enrollment quotas and propose budget needed to meet those goals; departments identify needs and establish priority lists linked to goals and objectives in 5-year plan; these proposals go from department to dean to vice president; budget presented to board of trustees in spring; sent to county legislature for adoption in July or August.

New Program Decision Process: If idea is generated by faculty member, it flows through a faculty senate process, described as a "braided" process. Once the proposal has been worked through the senate committees, it goes to the dean, and then the vice president. At each stage it goes back for further refinement; this back and forth process produces the "braided" effect.

Mt. San Antonio College

Location: Walnut, California
Founded: 1946
Credit Enrollment: 22,272
Board of Trustees: 5 member board, elected to 4-year terms (two elected one year, three elected the succeeding odd year)
President: John D. "Jack" Randall (acting president [during our site visit]: Joseph M. Zagorski).
Organization: single campus; title of CEO: Superintendent-President.
Faculty: 306
Administrators: 61
Classified Staff: 303
Annual Budget: $56 million
Collective Bargaining: Faculty Association (affiliated with California Teachers Association), California School Employees Chapter 262, and California School Employees Chapter 651.
Philosophy and Values:

> The Mt. San Antonio Community College District is dedicated to serving a diversified and changing population through excellence in teaching and in support services. The College, as an integral part of the community, meets the educational needs and aspirations of the people it serves. The primary purpose of Mt. San Antonio College is to offer high quality, comprehensive, and flexible programs designed to develop personal, academic, and/or job-related skills to all

adult members of the Mt. San Antonio College District and to those especially qualified by law who are able to benefit from the programs and services" [*Catalogue*, 1987–88, p. 1].

Leadership strength does not guarantee quality. Quality is directly related to the ideas and focused energies of people. In order to develop these energies, college leadership must establish a climate and participatory structure that brings out the enthusiastic and best involvement of faculty, staff, administrators, and students. . . . At Mt. San Antonio College we measure quality in terms of student success and teaching excellence [Dr. John Randall, Superintendent/President].

College Governance Structure (key decision-making groups):
- Board of Trustees (meets once a month; individually, trustees hold open meetings with staff, one board member each month of the school year—total of 10 per year).
- Administrative Council (president, two vice presidents, director, personnel, and dean, student services) (meets weekly).
- College Council (members of Administrative Council; president and president-elect, Faculty Senate; president, Faculty Association; one division dean; president, Associated Students; president, CSEA-262; and president, CSEA-651) (meets twice a month). The College Council and the Faculty Senate review all recommendations from committees before they go to the Administrative Council, the College President, or the Board of Trustees. The College Council may send recommendations back to committees for further study, with suggestions. College council minutes reflect the disposition of the recommendations from the committees. . . . Items for the College Council agenda may be submitted through the following sources: Administrative Council, Faculty Association, Faculty Senate, Classified representative, associated students, and college committees.

• Faculty Senate: Elect one or two per department (total 40+). Senate meets every Thursday. Senate makes all faculty appointments to committees. Executive Council (5 members, Faculty Association holds seat *ex officio)* meets every Monday, sets agenda for senate meeting. Six standing committees (Structure and Governance, Academic Affairs, Student Relations, Professional Relations, Vocational, Affirmative Action).

• Faculty Association: Representative Council (one from every department of 10 or fewer faculty, two from every department with more than 10); the entire membership elects the executive board: 4 officers, 8 directors, 1 collective bargaining negotiator; 8 standing committees; bargaining team of 3–7 members—216 clock hours released time (per year) distributed among team members.

• College committees: 31 in 1988–89 (for example, Accreditation, Campus Master Plan, Computer Services Advisory, Mission and Goals, President's Advisory-Budget, Support Personnel Staff Development).

Budget Decision Process: Departments review current budget, may reallocate within. Requests for additional monies submitted to department chairs and division deans, who prioritize and submit to the business manager. The Budget Committee (Administrative Council augmented by accounting department representative) reviews requests prepared by business manager and determines level of spending. Budget Committee builds in board standards, such as a 5 percent operational reserve, and other objectives reported through the superintendent. Each budget control officer may meet with Budget Committee to review requests and provide rationale (tied to college goals). The President's Advisory Committee-Budget (PAC-B) (broadly representational of constituent groups) reviews budget in general terms, discusses priorities identified by the Budget Committee. PAC-B is primarily a communicating, not a deciding, group. After this process is complete, recommended budget taken to board of trustees for action.

Hiring Decision Process: Philosophy as stated by one college leader, "Hiring is the most important thing we do. Hire the right people, everything else goes well." Once position is authorized, departments recruit with attention to gender and ethnic balance. Applications are screened by a committee chaired by division dean with faculty elected by department. All candidates for interview must submit a writing sample and present a teaching demonstration. The committee recommends two candidates per position for interview by president and vice president. Consultation with division dean and department chair for final choice by the president to be recommended to board of trustees.

Santa Barbara City College

Location: Santa Barbara, California
Founded: 1909 (discontinued after World War I, reestablished in 1946)
Credit Enrollment: 11,602
Board of Trustees: 7-member board representing trustee areas, elected at large to four-year terms.
President: Peter MacDougall
Organization: single campus; title of CEO: Superintendent/ President
Faculty: 181
Administrators/Management: 41
Classified Staff: 205
Annual Budget: $29,221,601
Collective Bargaining: Instructors' Association (unaffiliated), first contract completed January 1987; California School Employees Association, Chapter 289
Philosophy:

> Guiding Principles: . . . There is in each individual an intrinsic dignity and worth. . . . A democratic society functions best when its members are educated and participating citizens. . . . Individuals have the capacity to learn to direct

their destiny and the responsibility to participate effectively in the affairs of society. . . . The opportunity to learn should be accessible to all who can profit from it and who wish to avail themselves of it. . . . Each person should be encouraged and helped to realize his/her fullest potential regardless of economic, educational, or physical disadvantages, and/or cultural differences. . . . The community and the individual are best served when people can find satisfying and productive vocations and can learn to make rewarding use of leisure time. . . . It is important that all people learn about cultural heritages and how to work together to create a better society. . . . As a community college, Santa Barbara City College must be responsive to the needs of the community it serves. . . . A commitment to the ideal and tradition of academic freedom is basic to an intellectual environment which encourages serious scholarship and critical, independent thinking. . . . Education is a lifelong process—not solely preparation for adult life" [*Faculty Manual*, 1988, pp. 1-2].

District Governance Structure (key decision-making groups):
   • Board of Trustees: "The functions of the Board of Trustees shall be legislative, and it shall act as a policy-forming body. It shall consider questions of general educational policy and shall place the responsibility for implementation of Board adopted policies directly in the hands of the District Superintendent as executive officer of the Board" (*Faculty Manual*, p. 4). Three board committees: Educational Policies, Facilities, Fiscal (meets twice monthly).
   • President's Cabinet: President, 5 vice presidents (meets weekly).
   • College Planning Council: Cabinet plus 3 division chairs, academic senate president, classified representative, and student representative. Prepares Statement of Institutional

Directions, reviews 5-year plans from all units, and advises superintendent/president on fiscal/planning matters.

• Continuing Education Advisory Board: 40-member group that develops recommendations regarding continuing education and noncredit programs.

• Academic Senate: "All certificated employees of the District who do not perform any services for the college that require an administrative or supervisory credential" (*Faculty Manual*, 1988, p. 9). Representative Council (president and 14 faculty elected from the Academic Senate). Standing Committees: Academic Freedom and Professional Standards, Faculty Enrichment, and Sabbatical Leave.

• Instructors' Association: Contract focused on salary, benefits, and grievance process. Waived other rights, keeping existing senate and college committee structure functioning as in past.

• College Committees: 17 committees, such as Facilities Planning, Division Chair Council, Student Services Advisory, Intersegmental Advisory, Computer Assisted Instruction. *Budget Decision Process:* In retreat with superintendent/president, board sets large parameters for entire budget (criteria such as safety and 5% operating reserve are established). All departments review and revise 5-year plans. Each division, after prioritizing department requests, submits a comprehensive plan (requests for staff, equipment, supplies, and so on). Budget development builds on a distillation of all 5-year plans, which is channeled through organizational units (Instruction, Student Services, Business, Continuing Education). This draft budget goes to College Planning Council (CPC) for review. Discussion, debate, and compromise occur in CPC based on presentations/recommendations from vice presidents. Council recommendations go to the president who makes final decisions on recommendations to be taken to board committees and finally the full board for approval.

Santa Monica College

Location: Santa Monica, California
Founded: 1929

Credit Enrollment: 20,939
Board of Trustees: 7 members, elected to 4-year terms, staggered so some expire in each even-numbered year
President: Richard Moore
Organization: single campus; CEO title: Superintendent-President
Faculty: 240
Administrators: 60
Classified Staff: 400
Annual Budget: $53 million
Collective Bargaining: Santa Monica College Faculty Association—three-year contract; California School Employees Association, Santa Monica Chapter 36—three-year contract.
Philosophy:

> Santa Monica College is a community-oriented, open-door, educational institution dedicated to the principle that society benefits when its members have an opportunity to develop to their fullest potentials. Students are recognized as individuals with the capacity to learn and the desire to understand themselves, their environment, their cultural heritage, and their democratic way of life.
>
> The educational program at Santa Monica College reflects the leadership of the Board of Trustees and the active participation of citizens of the community in college affairs. The curriculum is developed cooperatively by a faculty that recognizes teaching as its primary responsibility and an administration that encourages and recognizes creativity and excellence in instruction. The college believes that genuine achievement is based on high standards of performance that require reasonable self-discipline by students. To make this possible, faculty, administration and staff recognize the need for high quality educational support through library, counseling, finan-

cial aids, and other services to students. Also, because the college serves an extremely diversified community with varying needs and expectations, it offers quality programs to meet the needs of all students, including the disabled, disadvantaged, and underrepresented.

The instructional offerings of the college are designed to meet various community educational needs including the following objectives:

To provide courses of sufficient generality and depth to allow students to transfer to four-year college with adequate preparation for success;

To provide a wide range of curricula in occupational and technical fields leading directly to employment or a transfer program;

To provide programs to assist students to develop basic skills;

To provide both credit and noncredit courses that encourage exploration and help the student achieve a richer and more productive life;

To provide educational and cultural activities that contribute to the entire community [*Board Policy Manual*].

District Governance Structure (key decision-making groups):
- Board of Trustees (meets monthly).
- General Advisory Board: 60-100 community members "interested in the concerns of the college." Purposes: (1) participate in various aspects of college activities; (2) become better informed about college; (3) interpret the college to the community. (Meets every other month; 12-member executive committee meets alternate months.)
- Senior Staff (superintendent, 3 deputy superintendents, 1 assistant superintendent, 1 vice president, and administrative dean, Educational Development) (meets weekly, though much informal contact daily).
- Collegewide Coordinating Council (CCC): deputy

superintendent, Education (chair); Three Presidents; 2 instructional deans; Student Services dean; assistant superintendent, Personnel; vice president, Students; Classified Forum president; student government president. Six divisional councils feed planning recommendations into CCC; senate and deans' council recommendations may move through CCC, as well.

- Deans' Council (all deans and assistant deans).
- Three Presidents (president, past president, and president-elect of the academic senate)—president consults with this group weekly on current issues.
- Academic Senate: about 40 representatives elected proportional to department size; executive committee of 15 (officers and committee chairs).
- Classified Forum: representative group for classified staff for issues outside the scope of collective bargaining. Based on work area, one representative for every 10 staff.
- Faculty Association (informal breakfast meetings with senate leadership to coordinate between faculty groups).
- California School Employees Association: Operations and Support Unit, Office Technical and Business Services Unit; Instructional Assistant and Paraprofessional Unit.
- Associated Student Body.

Budget Decision Process: Expenditures (operating) developed from department requests, based on past year's experience. Requests adjusted at division level based on allocation. Division requests adjusted by dean within allocation. Senior staff sets priorities among all requests. Based on Senior Staff priority setting, superintendent-president takes recommendations to the board of trustees for approval. Income and initial revenue allocations are developed from deputy superintendent estimates. Using these estimates, Senior Staff works out allocations to expenditure categories. Divisions and departments are given allocations.

Personnel Decision Process: Department initiates request for position. Each division council consolidates and ranks requests according to priorities. Collegewide Coordinating Council consolidates all division council requests, ranking them according to priorities (which are based on criteria that emerge from the group). The Senior Staff with superintendent determine allocation (total number of positions to be authorized). Superintendent takes recommendation to board based on priorities set by coordinating council.

Yosemite Community College District

Location: Modesto, California
Founded: 1921 (as Modesto Junior College District)
Credit Enrollment: 17,178
Board of Trustees: 7-member board elected from three trustee areas, elected to 4-year terms.
Chancellor: Thomas Van Groningen
Organization: multicollege (each college separate accreditation); title of District CEO—Chancellor
Colleges: 2, each headed by a president: Modesto, Columbia
Faculty: 255 (Modesto, 211; Columbia, 44)
Administrators: 32 (Modesto, 22; Columbia, 6; District, 4)
Classified Staff: 340
Annual Budget: $42 million
Collective Bargaining: Yosemite Faculty Association (unaffiliated); California School Employees Association
Philosophy:

> The Yosemite Community College District is a locally governed postsecondary educational institution dedicated to the principle that society will benefit when all persons within it have the opportunity for life-long learning. To that end, the Yosemite Community College District is committed to providing career development, skills improvement, and job retraining along with a full range of academic courses to broaden cultural, ethical, social and self awareness. In addition, Yosemite Community College District may introduce and provide for avocational, civic, and recreational pursuits. What is known is made available to students, and they are encouraged to

apply that knowledge to enhance the quality of relationships with others and life in general.

Based on this philosophy, Yosemite Community College District offers a wide variety of quality educational services through Modesto Junior College and Columbia College to serve the citizens of Stanislaus, Tuolumne, and parts of Calaveras, Merced, Santa Clara, and San Joaquin Counties [*Board Bylaws*].

District Governance Structure (key decision-making groups):
- Board of Trustees (meets monthly; special meetings as required).
- Cabinet: chancellor, 2 college presidents, 1 vice-chancellor, Educational Services, 2 assistant chancellors (Business Services, Personnel Services) (meets monthly).
- District Administrative Council: cabinet plus 8 others from the two campuses (deans of instruction and of students, associate deans); agendas published a week early for comment, summary of meeting distributed among management team and to senate and union presidents (meets off campus in members' homes monthly).
- District Council: chancellor's cabinet, plus 6 faculty, 3 classified staff, 1 mid-level manager and 1 student; addresses districtwide policy issues, using a consensus process, and makes recommendations to the chancellor. Chancellor either forwards recommendation to board of trustees or submits an alternate proposal, understanding that members of district council may address the board regarding the council's position. Each college has established a college council, with comparable representation and similar functions. Faculty and support staff receive either reassigned time or a stipend.
- Comprehensive Planning Process (described in detail in Chapter Three).
- Employer-Employee Relations Council: 5 union representatives and 3 district representatives meet as needed to deal with contractual interpretation issues.

Budget Decision Process: Chancellor and board formulate

planning assumptions and philosophical guidelines during a retreat in August. Guidelines are distributed directing the comprehensive planning process, which begins in early fall; first preliminary budget in December "very idealistic," "pie-in-the-sky," produces historical record of what people feel they need; president, deans, faculty, support staff, and student leadership (college council) establish priorities at college level; each of three cost centers (the two colleges and the district-level operation) integrate plans into a draft district budget; cabinet, with review by district council, develops revenue estimates and assumptions in April; expenditures are revised based on expected revenue with tentative budget to board of trustees by June.

Resource B:

Instruments Used in the Survey

STUDY OF INTERNAL GOVERNANCE
QUESTIONNAIRE

(*Instructions:* We are interested in your perceptions of the governance situation in your district. These questions are being asked of a number of key personnel in your district. All results will be reported as group data; individual questionnaires will not be reported on. No doubt some questions will require you to form an opinion on the basis of limited information or experience. Please make your most conscientious effort to respond to each question. Note that all questions should be answered from a *district-level* perspective).

My primary role in district level governance is:

_____ faculty (union)   _____ faculty (senate)
_____ classified staff   _____ district administrator
_____ district CEO   _____ campus administrator
_____ campus CEO   _____ trustee
_____ student trustee   _____ student

(*Check only ONE, please.*)

Part A. Issues

Every community college district faces a wide range of challenges and conflicts, problems and opportunities. In order to deal with these situations, each district board through its staff puts into place an organizational structure, adopts rules, regulations, and procedures, and designates individuals and groups to carry out those activities necessary for the district to accomplish its mission. Thinking over the past several years in your community college district, indicate which of the issues, problems, or challenges from the list below you believe your district has experienced. *Please circle the appropriate response.*

	Major issue or challenge					*Minor* issue or challenge				Not an issue	Don't know
1. Adequacy and stability of financial resources		5	4	3	2	1				0	00
2. Establishing priorities for internal allocation of financial resources among curriculum, compensation, facilities, and equipment needs		5	4	3	2	1				0	00
3. Overall enrollment declines		5	4	3	2	1				0	00
4. Overall enrollment growth		5	4	3	2	1				0	00
5. Shifts in enrollment among program areas		5	4	3	2	1				0	00
6. Changes in student characteristics (for example, academic preparation, demographics)		5	4	3	2	1				0	00
7. Changes in community characteristics (for example, economics, demographics)	5	4	3	2	1					0	00
8. Competition for students											

from neighboring districts	5	4	3	2	1	0	00
9. Changes in state regulations and requirements	5	4	3	2	1	0	00
10. Maintaining high quality instructional ser- vices to students	5	4	3	2	1	0	00
11. Maintaining high quality sup- port services to students	5	4	3	2	1	0	00
12. Maintaining appropriate bal- ance among transfer, voca- tional and com- munity service programs	5	4	3	2	1	0	00
13. Maintaining quality of physical plant	5	4	3	2	1	0	00
14. Maintaining effective balance between part-time and full-time staff	5	4	3	2	1	0	00
15. Maintaining high staff morale	5	4	3	2	1	0	00
16. Maintaining high commitment of staff to achiev- ing district mission	5	4	3	2	1	0	00

17. Conflict between (or among) faculty and staff organizations, administration, and trustees	5	4	3	2	1	0	00
18. Controversy in the local community concerning issues related to your community college district	5	4	3	2	1	0	00
19. Competition between (or among) campuses in your district	5	4	3	2	1	0	00
20. Conflict between campuses and district administration	5	4	3	2	1	0	00
21. Balancing allocation of resources between (or among) campuses and district administration	5	4	3	2	1	0	00
22. Coordination of curriculum within the district	5	4	3	2	1	0	00

If you wish, list up to three issues, problems, or challenges your district has faced that were not addressed in the list above.

23._____
_____
_____ 5 4 3 2 1   0   00

24._____

_____   5   4   3   2   1   0   00

25._____

_____   5   4   3   2   1   0   00

Part B. Successes

Obviously not all of the issues above are totally within the control of your college district. Acknowledging such limitations and constraints, indicate how successfully you feel these issues have been dealt with.

	Very success- fully			Very unsuccess- fully		Not applicable	Don't know
1. Adequacy and stability of finan- cial resources	5	4	3	2	1	0	00
2. Establishing priorities for inter- nal allocation of financial resources among curricu- lum, compensa- tion, facilities, and equipment needs	5	4	3	2	1	0	00
3. Overall enroll- ment declines	5	4	3	2	1	0	00
4. Overall enroll- ment growth	5	4	3	2	1	0	00
5. Shifts in enroll- ment among pro- gram areas	5	4	3	2	1	0	00

6. Changes in student characteristics (for example, academic preparation, demographics)	5	4	3	2	1	0		00
7. Changes in community characteristics (for example, economics, demographics)	5	4	3	2	1	0		00
8. Competition for students from neighboring districts	5	4	3	2	1	0		00
9. Changes in state regulations and requirements	5	4	3	2	1	0		00
10. Maintaining high quality instructional services to students	5	4	3	2	1	0		00
11. Maintaining high quality support services to students	5	4	3	2	1	0		00
12. Maintaining appropriate balance among transfer, vocational and community service programs	5	4	3	2	1	0		00

13. Maintaining quality of physical plant	5	4	3	2	1	0	00
14. Maintaining effective balance between part-time and full-time staff	5	4	3	2	1	0	00
15. Maintaining high staff morale	5	4	3	2	1	0	00
16. Maintaining high commitment of staff to achieving district mission	5	4	3	2	1	0	00
17. Conflict between (or among) faculty and staff organizations, administration, and trustees	5	4	3	2	1	0	00
18. Controversy in the local community concerning issues related to your community college district	5	4	3	2	1	0	00
19. Competition between (or among) campuses in your district	5	4	3	2	1	0	00
20. Conflict between campuses and district administration	5	4	3	2	1	0	00

21. Balancing
allocation of
resources between
(or among) cam-
puses and district
administration   5   4   3   2   1   0   00
22. Coordination
of curriculum
within the district   5   4   3   2   1   0   00

If you chose to list other issues in Part A, list those same issues here and indicate how successfully you feel your district has dealt with them.

23._____
_____
_____   5   4   3   2   1   0   00
24._____
_____
_____   5   4   3   2   1   0   00
25._____
_____
_____   5   4   3   2   1   0   00

Part C. Role of Governance

Now we would like you to think about what role *district-level* governance has played in dealing with the issues listed above. For purposes of this study, *governance is defined as structures and processes for district-level decision making and communication.* In considering your responses, focus on such important governance decisions as resource allocation, policy making, and policy implementation, not on individuals or personalities. With these considerations in mind, indicate the role district-level governance has played in dealing with the issues listed.

	Major role				No role	Not applicable	Don't know
1. Adequacy and stability of financial resources	5	4	3	2	1	0	00
2. Establishing priorities for internal allocation of financial resources among curriculum, compensation, facilities, and equipment needs	5	4	3	2	1	0	00
3. Overall enrollment declines	5	4	3	2	1	0	00
4. Overall enrollment growth	5	4	3	2	1	0	00
5. Shifts in enrollment among program areas	5	4	3	2	1	0	00
6. Changes in student characteristics (for example, academic preparation, demographics)	5	4	3	2	1	0	00
7. Changes in community characteristics (for example, economics, demographics)	5	4	3	2	1	0	00
8. Competition for students from neighboring districts	5	4	3	2	1	0	00

9. Changes in state regulations and requirements	5	4	3	2	1	0	00
10. Maintaining high quality instructional services to students	5	4	3	2	1	0	00
11. Maintaining high quality support services to students	5	4	3	2	1	0	00
12. Maintaining appropriate balance among transfer, vocational and community service programs	5	4	3	2	1	0	00
13. Maintaining quality of physical plant	5	4	3	2	1	0	00
14. Maintaining effective balance between part-time and full-time staff	5	4	3	2	1	0	00
15. Maintaining high staff morale	5	4	3	2	1	0	00
16. Maintaining high commitment of staff to achieving district mission	5	4	3	2	1	0	00
17. Conflict between (or							

among) faculty
and staff organiza-
tions, administra-
tion, and trustees   5   4   3   2   1   0   00

18. Controversy in
the local commu-
nity concerning
issues related to
your community
college district   5   4   3   2   1   0   00

19. Competition
between (or
among) campuses
in your district   5   4   3   2   1   0   00

20. Conflict
between campuses
and district
administration   5   4   3   2   1   0   00

21. Balancing
allocation of
resources between
(or among) cam-
puses and district
administration   5   4   3   2   1   0   00

22. Coordination
of curriculum
within the district 5   4   3   2   1   0   00

If you chose to list other issues in Part A, list those same issues here and indicate what role you feel district-level governance has played in dealing with those issues.

23._____

_____

_____   5   4   3   2   1   0   00

24._____

_____
_____ 5   4   3   2   1   0   00

25._____

_____
_____ 5   4   3   2   1   0   00

Part D. Comments

ASCCC/CEO/CCCT* STUDY OF
INTERNAL GOVERNANCE

Interview Guide

Introduction. We are here because your district volunteered to participate in a study of governance processes in community colleges sponsored jointly by the statewide Academic Senate, the statewide CEO organization, and the statewide trustees' organization. From among the districts that volunteered, your district was selected by a steering committee representing trustees, administrators, and faculty as a district which reflected better than average success with several major issues facing community colleges and which attributed some part of that success to its governance processes.

Purpose. Our intention in interviewing you is to get as complete a picture as possible in the limited time we have of what structures your district uses for decision making, how those structures function, and what communication processes are employed in relation to decision making. Rather than approach these questions in the abstract, we will ask you to describe how they operate in relation to some specific kinds of decisions and situations.

Our purpose is primarily descriptive, not evaluative. However, all responses will be kept confidential. We will be combining your responses with those of others in your institution. No individual response will be reported; rather the data we gather will be summarized as reflecting the perspective of a trustee, an administrator, or a faculty member (or student or staff member or community member, if appropriate).

*Academic Senate of the California Community Colleges/ Chief Executive Officers/California Community College Trustees

Overview

0. To give us a general picture of your district decision-making structures and processes, please name the groups or organizations (from the department level to the board level, in or out of your formal organizational structure) who participate in district-level decision making.

    0.1 What are the numbers in each group?

    0.2 What are the titles of group members?

    0.3 What formal relationships exist between the groups?

    0.4 When are decisions made in the groups based on presentations and discussion? When do participants come to the group with positions representing constituencies?

Case One: Budget Development Questions

Every year each community college must build a budget. Various individuals and groups participate in this process up to final adoption by the board of trustees. Help us understand who participates, how they participate, at what point(s) in the process, and in what situations.

1. Name the groups or organizations (from the department level to the board level, in or out of the formal organizational structure) who participate in your formal budget development process. Do all of these groups have official roles? Name any other groups that play unofficial roles in the process.

    1.1 What are the numbers in each group?

    1.2 What are the titles (or roles) of group members?

    1.3 Who selects group members? How are they selected?

    1.4 How frequently do these groups meet?

    1.5 Over what period of time do these groups deal with the budget?

1.6 Describe the role that each group plays in budget decision making: propose, recommend, analyze, review, refer, decide (select as many as apply).

(*Prompt:* if not yet mentioned, ask about role of unions and bargaining agents.)

2. Name those individuals who participate in your budget development process as individuals, independent of their role in any of the groups described already. Which participate formally? Which informally?

2.1 What are the titles (or roles) of those individuals?

2.2 How frequently do these individuals contribute?

2.3 Over what period of time do these individuals deal with the budget?

2.4 Describe the role that each individual plays in budget decision making: propose, recommend, analyze, review, refer, decide (select as many as apply).

3. At what stages in your budget development process are competing or conflicting proposals resolved?

3.1 Who participates in the resolution of competing or conflicting proposals?

3.2 What written procedures, if any, guide or constrain the resolution process?

3.3 What circumstances lead to the conflict's being referred to another level of the organization (either up or down)?

4. If it has not yet emerged, what relation does the budget development process have to collective bargaining with employee organizations?

Case Two: Priorities for New and Replacement Positions

Throughout the year, vacancies occur in staff positions, requiring a decision about replacement. Concurrently, various departments and programs identify the need for new positions.

Help us understand how your district makes these staffing decisions.

5. Who (by title or role) participates in identifying the need for a replacement or a new staff position?

6. Once a replacement or new position is proposed, what steps are involved before a position is authorized?

> 6.1 Name the individuals (by title or role) and groups who participate at each step.
>
> 6.2 What is the range of authority (review, recommend, reject, refer, approve) at each step?

7. What procedures are employed to evaluate the merits of a proposed position relative to other such proposals?

> 7.1 Identify who participates in this process.
>
> 7.2 How are priorities developed from the evaluation process?

Case Three: What Happens When X Has a New Idea and Wants to Implement It?

In every vital organization, individuals put forth new ideas and seek to implement them. We are interested in your perception of what happens when individuals playing different roles in your district seek to implement a new idea. Put another way, what processes have you observed by which an individual's idea becomes institutionalized?

8. Think of an instance in which a district trustee offered a new proposal. Answer these questions:

> 8.1 What was the idea or proposal?
>
> 8.2 Where or with whom would the idea be tested (checked out)?
>
> 8.3 In what situation was it proposed? (Open meeting; committee; informal setting.)
>
> 8.4 If it was implemented, to whom (groups and/or individuals) was it referred for review and approval?
>
> 8.5 If it was not implemented, how was the decision reached? (Who was involved? What factors [operational, fiscal, political] contributed to the decision?)
>
> 8.6 Identify any ways in which you believe this decision process differs from the kinds of decisions made in Case One and Case Two.

9. Think of an instance in which a district administrator (or the district CEO) offered a new proposal. Answer these questions:

9.1 What was the idea or proposal?

9.2 Where or with whom would the idea be tested (checked out)?

9.3 In what situation was it proposed? (Open meeting; committee; informal setting.)

9.4 If it was implemented, to whom (groups and/or individuals) was it referred for review and approval?

9.5 If it was not implemented, how was the decision reached? (Who was involved? What factors [operational, fiscal, political] contributed to the decision?)

9.6 Identify any ways in which you believe this decision process differs from the kinds of decisions made in Case One and Case Two.

10. Think of an instance in which a faculty member (faculty leader?) offered a new proposal. Answer these questions:

10.1 What was the idea or proposal?

10.2 Where or with whom would the idea be tested (checked out)?

10.3 In what situation was it proposed? (Open meeting; committee; informal setting.)

10.4 If it was implemented, to whom (groups and/ or individuals) was it referred for review and approval?

10.5 If it was not implemented, how was the decision reached? (Who was involved? What factors [operational, fiscal, political] contributed to the decision?)

10.6 Identify any ways in which you believe this decision process differs from the kinds of decisions made in Case One and Case Two.

Case Four: Recent Crisis (Past Two Years)

Every organization faces unexpected, unpredictable situations that call for decisions under pressure. Such situations may arise from elements external to the organization (from the community, state, or government agencies) or they may arise from elements within the organization (for example, unexpected enrollment drop; mishandling of funds). Help us to understand how you perceive your district decision processes when faced with such a crisis.

11. Identify a crisis that your district has faced in the past two years. (Note: it need not be earthshaking, but it should be significant enough that the district's decision-making processes were engaged in some way.)

11.1 In what way did the crisis come to the attention of decision makers?

11.2 Who was informed about the crisis? In what order? At what time?

11.3 What unusual steps or procedures were employed in addressing the crisis? (e.g., special meetings; exceptions to policy; use of consultants or other ad hoc advisors)

11.4 What ordinary decision-making steps or procedures were used in addressing and resolving the crisis?

11.5 How was the crisis resolved?

11.6 Which processes involved (both usual and unusual) were most instrumental in reaching resolution?

11.7 Which processes involved (both usual and unusual) would you avoid in facing a similar situation in the future?

Assessment Questions

Based on your experience in this district, you probably have formed some views about what elements in your decision-making structures and processes make a difference.

12.1 What in your structures and processes for decision making is working well?

12.2 Where do the conflict points in the process usually appear?

12.3 What weaknesses do you see in your decision-making processes.

References

Bensimon, E. M. "The Meaning of 'Good Presidential Leadership': A Frame Analysis." *Review of Higher Education,* 1989, *12* (2), 107–123.

Bergquist, W. H., and Armstrong, J. L. *Planning Effectively for Educational Quality: An Outcomes-Based Approach for Colleges Committed to Excellence.* San Francisco: Jossey-Bass, 1986.

Birnbaum, R. *How Colleges Work: The Cybernetics of Academic Organization and Leadership.* San Francisco: Jossey-Bass, 1988.

Bolman, L. G., and Deal, T. E. *Modern Approaches to Understanding and Managing Organizations.* San Francisco: Jossey-Bass, 1984.

Brandt, S. C. *Entrepreneuring: The Ten Commandments for Building a Growth Company.* Menlo Park, Calif.: Addison-Wesley, 1982.

Breneman, D. W., and Nelson, S. C. "The Community College Mission and Patterns of Funding." In G. Vaughan (ed.), *Questioning the Community College Role.* New Directions for Community Colleges, no. 32. San Francisco: Jossey-Bass, 1980, pp. 73–81.

Burns, J. M. *Leadership.* New York: Harper & Row, 1978.

The Carnegie Foundation for the Advancement of Teaching. "Community Colleges: A Sector with a Clear Purpose." *Change,* 1990, *22* (3), 23–26.

Cohen, A. M., and Brawer, F. B. *The American Community College.* San Francisco: Jossey-Bass, 1982.

Cohen, M., and March, J. *Leadership and Ambiguity.* New York: McGraw-Hill, 1974.

Deegan, W. L., and Gollattscheck, J. F. (eds.). *Ensuring Effec-*

tive Governance. New Directions for Community Colleges, no. 49. San Francisco: Jossey-Bass, 1985.

DePree, M. *Leadership Is an Art.* East Lansing: Michigan State University Press, 1987.

Drucker, P. *Management: Tasks, Responsibilities, Practices.* New York: Harper & Row, 1974.

Eells, W. C. *The Junior College.* Boston: Houghton Mifflin, 1931.

Evaluation Team Representing the Commission of Higher Education of the Middle States Association of Colleges and Schools. *Report to the Faculty, Administrators, Staff, Trustees, and Students of Monroe Community College.* Philadelphia, Pa.: Middle States Association of Colleges and Schools, 1985.

Fryer, T. W., Jr. *Part One: Institutional Causes of Individual Irresponsibility.* Berkeley: Center for Studies in Higher Education, University of California, 1982.

Galagan, P. "Bringing Spirit Back to the Workplace: An Interview with Matthew Juechter." *Training and Development Journal,* Sept. 1988, *37,* 35–37.

Gardner, J. *The Tasks of Leadership. Leadership Papers/2.* Washington, D.C.: Independent Sector, 1986.

Giamatti, A. B. *A Free and Ordered Space: The Real World of the University.* New York: Norton, 1988.

Grand Jury, County of Alameda. *Final Report, 1988–1989.* Oakland, Calif.: County of Alameda, 1989.

Gulassa, C. M. "Budget Policy and Development Committee." In T. Fryer (ed.), *The Foothill-De Anza Papers.* Los Altos Hills, Calif.: Foothill-De Anza Community College District, 1985.

Gulassa, C. M. "Collaborative Governance in the Foothill/De Anza Community College District." In *Management Report 1988–89/3.* Cupertino, Calif.: Association of California Community College Administrators, 1989.

Havel, V. "Letter to Dr. Gustav Husak, General Secretary of the Czechoslovak Communist Party." In J. Vladislav, *Vaclav Havel: Living in Truth.* London: Faber and Faber, 1986.

Havel, V. *Disturbing the Peace: A Conversation with Karel Hviz-dala.* New York: Knopf, 1990.

Kerr, C., and Gade, M. *The Guardians.* Washington, D.C.: Association of Governing Boards of Universities and Colleges, 1989.

Kieffer, C. F., and Senge, P. M. "Metanoic Organizations in the Transition to a Sustainable Society." In *Technological Forecasting and Social Change,* 1982, *22* (2), 69–84.

Kouzes, J. M., and Posner, B. Z. *The Leadership Challenge: How to Get Extraordinary Things Done in Organizations.* San Francisco: Jossey-Bass, 1987.

Lipset, S. M., and Wolin, S. S. (eds.). *The Berkeley Student Revolt: Facts and Interpretations.* Garden City, N.Y.: Anchor, 1965.

Osborn, F. P. *MCC Directs Its Future: Strategic Planning at Monroe Community College.* Rochester, N.Y.: Monroe Community College, 1986.

Packard, V. *The Pyramid Climbers.* New York: McGraw-Hill, 1962.

Peters, T., and Austin, N. *A Passion for Excellence: The Leadership Difference.* New York: Random House, 1985.

Peters, T., and Waterman, R. *In Search of Excellence.* New York: Harper & Row, 1982.

Richardson, R. C., Jr. *Reforming College Governance.* New Directions for Community Colleges, no. 10. San Francisco: Jossey-Bass, 1975.

Schön, D. *The Reflective Practitioner.* New York: Basic Books, 1983.

Selznick, P. *Leadership in Administration.* Berkeley: University of California Press, 1957.

Staw, B. "Organizational Psychology and the Pursuit of the Happy/Productive Worker." *California Management Review,* 1986, *28* (4), 40–53.

Strachey, L. *Queen Victoria.* New York: Harcourt Brace, 1921.

Tierney, W. G. "Organizational Culture in Higher Education: Defining the Essentials." *Journal of Higher Education,* 1988, *59* (1), 2–21.

Vaill, P. "The Purposing of High Performing Systems." *Organizational Dynamics,* Autumn 1982, 23–29.

Van Dyne, L. "A College That Believes in 'Community.' " *Change,* 1973, *5* (1), 52–55.

Vaughan, G. B. *The Community College Presidency.* New York: American Council on Education, 1986.

Watkins, E. *Work Time: English Departments and the Circulation of Cultural Value.* Stanford, Calif.: Stanford University Press, 1989.

Weick, K. E. "Educational Organizations as Loosely Coupled Systems." *Administrative Science Quarterly,* 1976, *21* (1), 1–19.

Yankelovich, D., and Harman, S. *Starting with the People.* Boston: Houghton Mifflin, 1988.

Zwerling, L. S. "The Miami-Dade Story." *Change,* 1988, *20* (1), 10–23.

Index